DOES MY

I0453818

UNIVERSE

AN OVERTHINKER'S GUIDE TO LIVING BEYOND THE ORDINARY

LOOK BIG

IN THIS?

Kate Angel

Does My Universe Look Big in This?
An Overthinker's Guide to Living Beyond the Ordinary

www.kateangel.com

Copyright © 2024 Kate Angel

All rights reserved
No portion of this book may be reproduced mechanically, electronically, or by any other means, including photocopying, without securing the advanced written permission of the author. Likewise, no portion of this book may be posted to a website or distributed by any other means without securing the advanced written permission of the author.

Limits of liability and disclaimer of warranty
This book is strictly for informational and educational purposes only. The author and the publisher shall not be liable for any misuse of the enclosed material. The author and the publisher do not guarantee that any one following these techniques, suggestions, tips, ideas, or strategies will be successful or healed. The author and the publisher shall have neither liability nor responsibility to anyone with respect to any loss or damage caused, or alleged to be caused, directly or indirectly, by the information or suggestions contained in this book.

Medical disclaimer
To the extent that any medical or health information is shared in this book, it is provided as an information resource only and is not to be used or relied on for any diagnostic or treatment purposes. Any such information does not constitute patient information, does not create any patient-physician relationship, and should not be used as a substitute for professional diagnosis and treatment.

Author photo credit: Tracey Murray Photography

Published by Made to Change the World™ Publishing
Nashville, TN

ISBN: 978-1-956837-43-8 Print—Amazon
      978-1-956837-45-2 Print—Ingram
      978-1-956837-44-5 ebook

Printed in the USA, Canada, Australia, and Europe

I would like to acknowledge the Ngunnawal people,
the traditional owners of the land on
which this book has been written.

I have felt their presence throughout this writing journey,
and I thank them with every ounce of love in my heart
for the wisdom they have infused into its pages.

To all of you out there who are playing small
for fear that you might shine too brightly,
feel too deeply, or be too much.

CONTENTS

ACKNOWLEDGMENTS

This book, my journey, and all that I think is important would not have happened without:

Deepak Chopra, for pushing my intellect further than I ever thought it could go.

Neale Donald Walsch, for having the courage to put himself and his message out there so that I could learn, gain wisdom, and muster the courage to do the same.

Ram Dass, for educating me, empowering me to change, and showing me that spirituality didn't have to be a serious venture.

Joe Dispenza and Esther, Jerry, and Abraham Hicks, for their magical messages that enchanted me and have made me want more and more and more ever since.

Kitty Flanagan, Judith Lucy, and the hundreds of women the world over who have stood in the spotlight to make people laugh; if you've got it, flaunt it because you sure as hell can't hide it forever.

Michael Leunig, for teaching me that there is no end to the ways in which we can perceive our reality.

Elizabeth Gilbert and Hugh van Cuylenburg, for courageously sharing their stories with the humour they so seamlessly blend in.

Julia Zemiro, for sharing her humour and her empathy with such elegance and genuineness that I want to be just like her. I can't think of a better person I would rather have as my role model.

Emily Fletcher, for her soul-inspiring meditation program that cleared the debris for me to become the highest possible version of myself.

Jonna Jinton whose art and film making are the epitome of beauty, love, and authenticity and remind me to always create from my own heart.

Marie Ange, for asking all the right questions, holding space, and being there to listen to the often unintelligible answers.

Every teacher I ever had who had the patience to let me expend my energy the way I needed to, often in class while they were trying to teach.

To my parents, for leaving their hands off the reins, allowing me to explore, and taking on the worry so that I didn't have to.

To Sally and Jon who were there at the beginning where so many of the real adventures happened.

To the group of kindred spirits at the book-writing bootcamp who helped me birth this book.

To all of my friends who have supported me in my learning journey and who have either consciously or subconsciously contributed to the content of this book.

To every human on the planet, for being my mirror and showing me myself.

And, finally, to Ross, Nicholas, and Liam for being there, for being unapologetically themselves, and not for a moment acting like I was anything but the best wife and mother in the world.

INTRODUCTION

I was a sensitive child. Maybe everyone is to begin with. I felt things deeply, and I lived in my imagination. I think those two often go hand in hand. I would cry for the kid who forgot to bring their lunch to school or for the bus driver when he drove past with no passengers. But I also wouldn't hesitate to stick my face into a cobwebbed hole if I believed there might be a secret portal to another dimension inside, which I usually did. I blended reality and fiction so effortlessly that when I wasn't getting into trouble for daydreaming or telling lies, I was immersed in a fantasy world that kept me occupied all day long. With so much distraction, I'm surprised I learned to read and write, but when I did, suddenly, I had one more channel through which I could express my delight, my fear, my angst, and my passion, and I couldn't get enough of the blue-lined paper and thick lead pencils and of the power I had to create. I would scribble words with chalk on the footpath, in the dirt in the backyard, and in the sand at the beach. I would use exclamation marks, uppercases, and ellipses to make my feelings known to the world, and I knew, without a doubt, that I was a storyteller.

Then I went to high school where I discovered that writing was not the freeform, creative venture I was used to. And neither were emotions. English in the 1980s was a very serious affair, and feelings didn't feature in the syllabus at all. Emotions were mortifying and to be avoided at all costs to avoid ridicule and rejection. In their place were serious classics to be read and very boring essays to be written about them. And it all had to be true. It was a slog. Writing lacked the imagination I was used to, and I struggled to stay interested. English became, by far, my least-favourite subject, so in response, I hid away my pens and my notepads, ashamed that I ever thought writing could be my calling.

At university, I dabbled for a while in acting as an outlet for my passionate nature. If I couldn't express my emotions as myself, perhaps I could express them as somebody else. I did that for as long as I could until the only people left in the troupe were those who wanted to make a serious go of the profession. Given my mediocre talent and only being there for the emotional outlet, I dropped out. With that went the last of my creativity and my love of storytelling. By then I had wholeheartedly adopted society's message that if you wanted to be an artist, you had to be shit-hot talented, committed, and competitive, and my experiences in high school and at university made evident that I was anything but. I loved storytelling to bits, but apparently, that wasn't enough.

So I fell into a role in IT, contracting with the federal government because it was available and I needed a job. If I couldn't express my true self and my passion, then the IT-government combo was one of the safest places on Earth I could hide given that there was so little in the way of emotion or freeform creativity in either of those to risk reminding me of who I really was. I closed the final door on the passionate me. I pushed what was left of my emotions so deep into my body that I was able to forget about them for over twenty years.

In 2012, however, my husband and I took our young family to live in Thailand on an extended holiday. I willingly left my culture and my work behind, and for six whole months, I was free to create a new identity for myself. I wore the same pair of shorts and t-shirt every day, I went to bed each night with salt water in my hair, I never wore makeup, and I rarely wore shoes. I started to drive slower, eat more mindfully, and talk less; the burning urge to achieve and tick boxes that had fuelled me for so long faded into the background. I spent hours each day in the jungle behind our house, daydreaming and talking to myself. And I started writing stories. With no thought or planning, the real me started to poke her head out of her cave and step into the daylight without the fear of being slammed with criticism. It's only looking back that I recognise I was reconnecting with my authentic self. At the time though, all I knew was that I was free and happy and in a nirvana-like state of bliss.

But then things started to unravel. We returned to Australia amidst illness, a death in the family, and workplace tensions that eventually led to me losing my contract. The contrast between the life I was returning to and the one I had just left in Thailand was so jarring that I couldn't reconcile the two identities. I did a long, slow metaphorical face plant into the pavement during which I lost interest in my work and spent my days on autopilot, only going through the motions without the motivation or desire to think differently. My privileged, middle-class existence felt inadequate. I stopped enjoying the things I used to love, wondering whether I had ever liked them. I started questioning everything about my life. Despite all that, only a handful of those closest to me had a sense of what was going on because I was so au fait at playing the role of the perfect employee, daughter, sister, mother, wife, friend. I even claimed to my family doctor that I was "doing just fine" because I had nothing physically wrong with me, and I was doing decently well at keeping my shit together to fake it. I figured that "I'm bored with life" wasn't a clinical enough condition to warrant the use of valuable healthcare resources. This malaise was so chronically pervasive that it was easy for it to go unnoticed in the sea of people feeling the same way, passed off as a fact of life to be endured. When I finally skidded ungracefully to a halt and pulled myself up out of the dirt, it was 2022, and ten years had gone by.

There are many names for that type of malaise: Mid-life crisis, dark night of the soul, perimenopause, maybe even depression of sorts, and all of these are commonly seen as something negative to "endure as best you can." But I wasn't willing to accept that this was just some unfortunate condition to be fixed and put behind me as quickly as possible. My brief exposure to Buddhism in Thailand had planted the seed that everything has a reason, and so I decided to explore what was going on for me rather than ignore it. Buddhism led me to Hinduism, which led me to meditation. I read the Bhagavad Gita and the Kybalion, and I researched the laws of the universe, manifesting, energetics, philosophy, psychology, and quantum mechanics. I listened to podcasts, masterclasses, and YouTube channels on spirituality and the science of higher consciousness. I looked into indigenous cultures and listened to what they had to say about the same set of symptoms I was experiencing, and I adopted a term that, to me, carried a much more positive energy, which was, "Spiritual Awakening." Just saying it made me feel better. The idea that my spirit—my true self and the greater part of me—was coming to the surface gave me a sense of purpose and excitement. I integrated what I was learning into the way I lived, guided by my feelings and boosted by the confidence that came with knowing that this was all for the higher good. And I started to give myself long overdue permission to listen to what I really wanted and to muster the courage to take it.

It was through this process that I came to realise that emotions are the foundation of the entire life experience. Without them, there is no meaning, no beauty, no depth or richness. Not only that, but emotions are one of the best tools for living a truly extraordinary life. Most Westerners don't even realise that when paid attention to, emotions guide you toward your soul purpose and connect you with your highest self. Instead, you are taught to push them aside, ignore them, and hide them so they can't be seen or felt. Is it any wonder there is so much fear and unhappiness and turmoil in the world?

From my corporate world perspective, I have watched the epidemic of emotionlessness infect the people around me, and I have seen first-hand how this hinders the solutions needed for some of society's biggest problems. Since there is no point waiting for the government to do something about it—I am in the government—I decided to do something about it myself. I created Your Light Side to connect people with their authentic selves and their sense of fun and to leverage their biggest asset, their feelings, to live extraordinary lives.

In December 2023, I came across a writing workshop, an idea that lit me up so intensely that I signed up immediately, paid in full, and flew to the United States two weeks later to participate. It was a pivotal moment for me even though many people in my life thought I had finally lost the plot. I knew though, without a doubt, that this was just the real me accepting my truth and finally receiving what the universe had been trying to give me all along.

This book is the product of that workshop in California. It is for anybody whose emotional alarm is going off and whose spirit is awakening. It's about reconnecting with who you once knew you were and with the authentic person you wish to be. It's not about leaving your job, your family, or your hometown to find yourself. It's about inserting more of the real you into all of these spaces. It's time to poke your head out of your hole and take the morsels the universe has been patiently holding out for you so that it can finally relax and say, "Thank fuck she finally did it." It's actually also about having a good laugh.

It is my heartfelt intention that by reading this book you will recognise yourself as someone who is called to take this leap into your own authenticity, and we can then hang out together to revel in the amazing reality that we have discovered for ourselves. Along the way, you will realise there is nothing wrong with the life you have chosen, that it doesn't have to change for you to experience the richness that most people are oblivious to because they mistakenly think that what they experience is all there is. There is so much more colour and dimensionality and enjoyment to be had if you give yourself permission to feel it. This book is my deepest desire to connect with you and the many others who ache for more. I wish I had known you when I first started my own journey, but you're here now and I'm excited to bits.

CHAPTER 1

ENGAGE

GETTING STARTED

Sometimes, I can be a bit awkward when I'm introduced to people for the first time. It doesn't show; I've been assured by friends who know me well. I pull it off with finesse, apparently. But on the inside, there's doubt about whether I'm doing it right. Have I pronounced your name correctly? Am I talking too loudly? Have I just hugged you without first finding out whether you're the hugging type? Am I behaving *normally* enough? That it doesn't happen all the time stumped me. So I thought long and hard about why things were so weird with some people and not with others. And I realised it wasn't other people making me feel uncomfortable, it was me. When I showed up as myself, as my real authentic self, and stood solidly in my own truth with no masks, no pretending, and no role playing, I was at my most confident. When I first came to this realisation, I thought, "What?! That's the most counterintuitive thing I've ever heard! Don't we do all that pretending and faking to feel confident? Because our true selves make us feel awkward and uncomfortable and should be hidden?" Turns out, no, it's the opposite.

Social commentator and cartoonist Michael Leunig summed this up perfectly when he published a cartoon depicting a group of people sitting on a train under a sign that says, "Non Farting." On the other side of the train is a group of people sitting under a "Farting" sign. The group in the non-farting section is depicted as hunched over, drab, looking dejected. The people in the farting section are sitting confidently upright with cheeky glints in their eyes, like the world is their oyster and they've got nothing to hide. It's funny because it's the opposite of how most people think they ought to behave to be happy.

While you wear your protective armour, nobody can smell your farts or sense your vulnerability. But they also can't see you or connect with you, and you can't connect with them. The desire to connect with people is a significant driver in life, but the fear of rejection holds most people back. Together these can trap you in a loop of inaction. When you find the courage to show up as your truest self, however, you are free to connect deeply with others in a genuine way. This courage also gives you the confidence to withstand the fear that some of these connections will not turn out as you expect. Allowing yourself to be honest about who you really are opens you up to experiencing life in all of its full-blown technicolour beauty, uninhibited by heavy armour and the pretence of being someone you're not. And, yes, you have to accept the risk of a little cheek squeak slipping out—you know, the sorts of scenarios where you lose yourself in a moment of road rage in front of a first date or you misread a colleague's readiness to hear that you like to eat cat food. There are trade-offs to holding yourself back and there are trade-offs to showing up with courage, but those are your only choices, and you get to decide which way you're going to live.

Authenticity is following what excites you. When you were very little, this was the only way you knew how to be. Then, as you started thinking your way through life rather than flowing with nature, you got distracted by all the reasons to be inauthentic, and living by these constraints became your game. Living authentically is synonymous with freedom, happiness, and your soul's purpose—all of which are elusive when perceived from the limiting mindset of inauthenticity. In this book, I'm going to invite you to open your mind and see the world differently. I'll share some wild and undomesticated ideas, dare you to explore yourself from varying perspectives, and encourage you to take responsibility for things you've always believed you had no control over.

Discovering your own authenticity is a messy, haphazard process, the way backpacking was before the Internet and online banking. There is no formula, and it's definitely not linear. Being your authentic self is a moment-by-moment decision where you discover you are being more and more authentic more and more of the time. The chapters in this book are intended to spark your imagination, to make you question what you know and who you think you are, and, most importantly, to find out who you want to be. In any order.

THE CURRENT STATE

In IT project management, we like to do what's called a current-state analysis before we change anything. We do it before we design anything, build anything, implement anything. In fact, we do it before we make any move at all. A current-state analysis involves having a good old poke about the business environment to see what's there. It's like lifting rocks to see what beady-eyed creatures live underneath, opening filing cabinets, looking in drawers and lunchboxes, and writing lots of notes on a thick A4 clipboard. We check out what tools and processes people are using, what skills they have, and how they are organised. And we ask lots of probing, uncomfortable questions with no judgement. In reality, the no-judgement part doesn't always happen, but the aim is to form a narrative about the business landscape we are focussed on so that we can decide what we want to do next.

In standard practice, we write down facts and figures and dollar values and put them into a fancy report with funky graphics so that management can make a decision about what we have to do and how much it's going to cost. Additionally, when I do it, I observe how people feel. I look at how they behave, what they say, and their attitudes because these—not their skills, not the tools they use or processes they follow, or even the amount of money they have to do it all with—are the biggest influences when striving for improvement. Their feelings about where they are now and where they are going will make or break success.

Over the next three chapters, I invite you to do a current-state analysis on yourself. You are probably already sick to death of your own facts, figures, and funky pictures, so this is where you can find out what you've got going on at a deeper level that will, and already is, influencing where you want to go. It will take you beyond the logic of who you think you are by looking at how you feel, what you believe, and the way you experience your world.

CHAPTER 2

FEEL

FEELINGS AS EXPERIENCE

Have you ever asked somebody how they are, and they tell you the truth? And it's really weird because that's not actually what you were after? You just wanted them to say, "Good thanks," and be done with it?

I don't think emotions get nearly enough conscious airplay, especially given that they are responsible for how you experience the world. Emotions are like the chicken stock in the soup of life. Most times, when you're eating the soup, you don't even think about the stock, but that underlying flavour is always present.

My first memory of having an emotion was when I was told to stop having it. I was probably crying or laughing or something equally as unrestrained. When trying to teach kids some self-mastery, the lesson they often learn instead is: *Hold it in. You're too much. Don't take up so much space.* You're not really given instructions for how to do it either. You have to figure it out on your own. And, like most people, the way you learned to do it was to find somewhere in your body where you could shove all this emotion and hopefully forget about it until the end of time. Your body stores all of that repressed emotion. And by the time you get to your thirties, it is pretty full in there. All that repressed emotion from the past starts to seep out through the crevices in squeaks and farts and other unholy ways. It's not all bad emotions either. You've just been taught that it's bad. But there are some hidden gems in there that you would love to revisit if only you could find them again. In fact, much of that repressed emotion is your most exuberant, passionate self. You know, that loud, happy, joyful child who was so rambunctious that no one could handle it? It runs in my family, that exuberance. My grandmother had it. My mother's got it. In the family photo album, there is not a single photo of my mother as an infant where she wasn't standing up in her pram or her cot instead of lying down, where she wasn't on the move, the photo blurred because she'd already bolted. In fact, in the first photo I remember of her standing still, she's about six years old, and I'm betting that took some real restraint. There's a message in there for anyone who recognises themselves and wants to put that thought in their authenticity swag bag.

I'm going to call on a wise being, the newborn baby. Nigel the newborn is going to demonstrate this point. So Nigel is fresh out of the ether and onto the planet, and he possibly doesn't even know that he's incarnated again. He is just blissfully being. And all he's got at this stage are the inputs from his senses—sight, sound, touch, etc. And to him it's all just colours, movement, noise, shapes. None of it means anything because he hasn't learnt to put meaning to it yet. Nigel also feels sensations within his body. He feels that warm poo against his bum in his nappy. He feels that emptiness in his stomach, which is hunger, a sensation he hasn't learned to put any positive or negative meaning to. And, in fact, the less meaning he assigns it, the better.

Because when he's hungry his body is going to take care of that. His body's going to make some noise, and then the nipple's going to arrive and his body will know what to do with it. His body operates best when he has zero opinions about how it works or how it should be. His job is to blissfully enjoy the ride. But it doesn't take long before all that changes.

Soon enough, Nigel learns to assign meaning to events, thoughts, and sensations in the physical environment, and he joins the bigger kid's sandpit. When he smiles, it's a good thing and people clap. When he cries, it's a bad thing and people get sad. It's a momentous occasion, that first emotional attachment to something. It's a pity he can't identify it and frame it. "Baby's first neural pathway." It's a milestone. It's the very first step toward creating that filter that he'll use to navigate his way through life. And he needs a filter. There's too much going on in his internal and external environments to process it all at once. No wonder newborns always look so stunned.

So he starts to assign meaning to things, and that narrows down the environment to the stuff that matters, and it makes the world a lot more manageable. But it also starts to frame his perception of reality. Suddenly, he's eliminated a big slice of his truth, and it becomes invisible to him.

Nigel is you. Nigel is me. Nigel is everyone. If that wasn't obvious.

I was once in Bali with my mum, walking down a street in Ubud, and the traffic was awful—cars along the main tourist street were in constant gridlock; scooters accelerated in every direction; and the smell and the noise were so abrasive I couldn't enjoy myself. Every lungful I took felt like it was doing damage, and I was getting shittier and shittier. I finally couldn't stand it any more, and I said to my mum, "I can't keep going. This traffic is so effing effed it's giving me the effing shits." (Obviously, I didn't say it like that. The words I used weren't nearly as eloquent.) Anyway, my mother looked over at the road as if she was literally seeing it for the first time, and she said, "Gosh, I hadn't even noticed."

She lives in Sydney. It's a bigger place than my home, Canberra. They get traffic like that all the time, and she's filtered it out because it means nothing to her. But as a kid who used to get car sick, who sees smog as an environmental atrocity, and who has an aversion to driving because I can't reverse parallel park properly, I was more attuned to the traffic than someone for whom it has no meaning in their life.

Feelings affect what you focus on. Positive feelings make you focus on opportunities and are more likely to be associated with gratitude, constructive thinking, and creativity. Negative feelings make you focus on threats and cynicism, which are more likely to be associated with a scarcity mindset and emotional instability. What you feel in the here and now is your reality; it's the truth, it's your authentic self. So giving yourself permission to have feelings, and to acknowledge them, is an essential part of being your authentic self.

Remember your alter ego, Nigel? He grew up and had more experiences in the world; you would think that he learned to see *more*, but the truth is that he actually saw less. He took all those experiences and their associated emotions and tried to squeeze them into the narrative he developed at a fairly young age.

Does that resonate? The goal now isn't to continue to stuff more feelings into those crevices—it's to clear them out, to assess them honestly, and to figure out which of them are serving your authentic self. Your intention shouldn't be to feel less, it should be to feel more—more of the real stuff. This is how you start to tell a different story.

THE OVERRATED PASTIME OF THINKING

Feelings aren't just a function of your mind. They're a holistic and physically immersive experience. Every emotion you feel has a corresponding reaction in your body. Test it with excitement, and locate where you feel the rush. Where do you feel disappointment or disempowerment? Notice the sensations you experience throughout your body. Every emotion links to a corresponding group of chemicals and neurotransmitters. Some of the seemingly opposite emotions feel very similar in the body; so similar, in fact, that the only way you can differentiate them is by the context in which they occur.

Your heart's palpitating. You're jittery. You can feel the adrenaline squirting into your veins. The "I'm going to die" chemicals are coursing through your body. There's obviously a very strong emotion going on. You assess your surroundings; you are in the jungle face-to-face with a soldier in army fatigues with enormous muscles who is holding a machine gun. You're going to draw the conclusion that you're scared. On a different day, your blood is also pumping. Your heart rate is up. The same thing is happening in your body as happened in the jungle. You look around; you're face-to-face with the same man with the machine gun, but this time he's on the red carpet in Hollywood. You're seeing your favourite actor in the flesh for the first time having idolised him since you were a teenager. It's a rare and majestic moment, and he's looking right at you. You're going to conclude that you are super excited.

Context is everything when it comes to emotion, and that context is drawn from your opinions, your thoughts, and your beliefs—in essence, your thinking—about the world around you. The thinking that you insert into this entire melange is the active ingredient, and it's potent. It's so powerful, in fact, that you really want to think sparingly. It's kind of counterintuitive though, isn't it, to use thinking sparingly, given thinking is often considered the pinnacle of human ability?

"Think!!" I used to get told in school on a regular basis, usually when I had done something stupid. Thinking is put on a pedestal in mainstream culture. But these higher-order reasoning functions are the smallest and the youngest parts of the brain compared to the emotional centre, which is older, larger, and more intuitive. So when you put all your eggs in the thinking basket, you're, in fact, ignoring an enormous part of your inner wisdom.

Once, when I was at after school care when I was little, I saw a woman sitting on a bench crying. One of the other mothers sat down next to her. As I walked past, I heard the two of them talking. The mother comforting the crying woman was so relaxed in her ability to just *be* with this woman as she experienced whatever was going on for her. It was the first time I had seen emotion dealt with so calmly. No one was freaking out. There was no panic, no shame. It was just a relaxed conversation that didn't have an agenda. No one was trying to get anywhere. No one was trying to stop anything from happening or make something happen. I still remember the peace and awe that I felt as I looked on. In my own past, emotion had always been something stressful, something to worry about, something to be fixed. I was amazed that it could be dealt with in any other way.

Have you heard the saying, "It's not a problem, it's an emotion?" Emotions are allowed to be there. They're supposed to be. They are who you are, and when you ignore them, you ignore a large part of your truth and limit your ability to experience life. Your reactions to and opinions of your emotions also have a profound effect on how well you deal with them and how much you learn from what they tell you.

Back to the face-to-face encounter with the soldier in the jungle. You survived. But, now, every time you see a picture of a soldier or even somebody with a bald head, you go into full-on hysteria. After this has happened a couple of times, you get a bit fed up. Not only do you regularly feel the same fear you did back in the jungle, but you're really unhappy about the fact that you have to feel this fear repeatedly. Eventually, you feel perpetually disappointed because you anticipate that you will be unhappy because you're going to feel the fear again. Layers pile upon layers, which, over time, can obscure the real reason for your emotion. You respond to the top layer of emotion, the disappointment, as if it's the only reason. You say, "Soldiers annoy me. They are so lame," rather than describing the initial emotion: "I'm scared because a soldier almost killed me." The latter is a much more reasonable explanation for why you have such an exaggerated reaction to soldiers, but you don't recognize that and, instead, think of yourself as irrational.

The amount of time it takes for the emotional chemicals to dissipate in the body can be as little as ninety seconds in most cases. If you let an emotion play out without interrupting it, without having an opinion about it; if you just feel it and don't poke it again, then it too will dissipate, just like the chemicals. But often you don't get a chance to do this. Like many people, you may have been taught that you have to control yourself, and quickly, because, horror, somebody might see. You're taught this from a young age. Here comes the emotion . . . "Oh, no, people are going to get angry with me, or feel embarrassed, or be disappointed, or whatever, so shut it all down because having this type of emotion is inappropriate." But holding it in has consequences. It's not dissimilar to what you know about going to the toilet—that you should go when you need to go. But if it's not convenient, you might opt for the consequences—clench and hold it. It's the same with an emotion. You can't choose when you feel it. It can happen any old time—when you're at work, at the ballet, or at a family dinner—but because you're trying to stifle it, you get emotionally constipated.

Ironically, those "active ingredient" thoughts that you expect to make you function on a higher level are like emotional laxatives. Have the triggering thought and that entire emotional sequence comes gushing forth. They're very effective, those laxative-style thoughts. Even when you've decided, "That's it! I'm giving up! No more laxatives!" your brain sneaks them into a cheese cube in your dinner bowl, and the next thing you know, you're thinking about soldiers all day long even though that's the last thing you want. Think the same thought-emotion sequence often enough, and your body programs the recurring emotion into autopilot so that you can experience it on an endless loop even without the laxative. It's like Microsoft Help saying, "We've noticed you complete this action frequently. Let us help you save some time." The body is a programmable instrument which literally programs itself by repetition. The more often you do something, the more automated it will become, and that's especially true for feeling emotions. The body's job is to use and conserve energy as efficiently as possible, so it simplifies recurring actions.

To continue the analogy (stay with me, it's almost over), you're provoking your emotions from the top end, but you're clenching to hold them in at the bottom end, and you're running out of space for them all. You're holding onto your lower colon for dear life, your stomach starts to hurt, and every muscle in your body tightens to hold all this stuff in. Even your throat gets sore because you're running out of places to store all this unsavoury emotion. Is it any wonder that you're starting to feel unwell?

In contrast, if you let yourself feel negative emotion from the start without assigning an opinion, without immediately suppressing it or halting it in its tracks, not only do you allow the emotion to pass completely through your body so that it's gone forever, but, amazingly, it doesn't hurt nearly as much. That opinion-thought you assigned to negative emotions is like rubbing salt into a wound. It's what generates a lot of the pain of those emotions. But if you park your opinion and give yourself permission to sit with the physical feeling of the emotion in your body—explore it, savour it, get to know it, figure out what it's trying to tell you without being in such a hurry to swipe left—then it becomes surprisingly manageable. If you haven't tried this already, I recommend giving it a go. It could change your life.

It's an insightful exercise when you first try feeling your emotions because you really get to know how you are currently managing them. I've always suppressed my sadness and my urge to cry. I learned to do this at an early age. It was a survival mechanism, especially in the schoolyard. Crying indicated to the mean kid that he had won. Tears broadcast my weaknesses to the world and provided those I couldn't trust with one more piece of ammunition for sinking me. As an adult though, for my own well-being, I decided to allow myself to cry more. I told myself that the next time I felt the need to cry, I was just going to let it happen. It would be part of my healing and discovery journey. I was really looking forward to it. It was going to be so therapeutic, such a nice, big release. So I watched a sad movie, and I could feel it coming. I thought, "Yes, this is it! Here we go. I'm really doing it." I gave myself permission, I let my eyes well up, my chest tightened, and suddenly . . . it was gone. I was like, "Where did it go?" Turns out, that's my body's learned response to crying. I've taught my body for so many years that crying needs to be shut down the moment it starts, that now when I want to cry, my body doesn't know how. It just blocks it in my chest. My body will need to learn that it's safe to cry, but for now, it's pretty sceptical. It's like a little marsupial poking its head out of its hole, checking for predators. I'm going to have to sit patiently with a morsel of food in my hand, waiting for it to trust me again.

There is also a difference between allowing yourself to feel an emotion and expressing it. Feeling is all about observing the sensation in your body without trying to stop it or change it. Expressing is the outward behaviour that results from the emotion. You're probably already thinking ahead to all the real, live, and possibly mortifying scenarios that could play out if you don't differentiate the two (or reliving the past real, live, and definitely mortifying scenarios that already played out). Depending on where you are and what company you're in, choosing how you express your emotions while still allowing yourself to feel and acknowledge them is a pretty amazing skill for the swag bag.

Sounds hard? Nah. Only if you believe it should be. No need to chug that fourth glass of overproof yet because the outlook is good. You can shift this stored emotion once and for all, and there's a blissful exercise at the end of this chapter where you get to use your imagination and your creativity to do it.

FEELINGS AS A GUIDE

After all the effort you put into your emotions, have you ever wondered what they are even for? It's easy to go down the Darwinian route and say that emotion is for survival, designed to keep you close to the pack and conforming to the group because being with the group is how you survive. You know the drill: If you're not like one of them, then you're going to be cast out into the wilderness and left to die. And you know what it's like to feel like you don't belong, that you're doing something inappropriate, or that you're not the right fit. And while that certainly explains why you can get so trapped by your emotions, I reckon you can do better than that. I think humans have reached a point in evolution where life can be more than just about staying alive. And assuming that's true, I'm going to take a quick existential tangent so that you'll understand where I'm coming from.

If life is about more than just survival, then that implies it has a purpose. I alluded to this before when I said that life is about self-discovery. That's your purpose. Your only job is to get to know yourself, and you do that by interacting with the world around you through your feelings. While you're at it, you evolve toward the best version of yourself to ultimately connect at a greater level with the wisdom of God, Spirit, Source, Creator, All That Is, or whatever term you like to use for the higher consciousness that is reflected all around you and within you. That's it in a nutshell. Regardless of what you are doing in life and what you think about what you are doing, your soul is ever evolving. Your soul has the plan, the evolutionary blueprint, the map from A to B. It is in the driver's seat and your human is just the vehicle along for the ride. You're going to learn all the lessons you're here to learn whether you want to or not. Evolution is a given. This might seem contradictory, especially since humanity as a whole appears to be doing a lot of devolving. But from a soul's perspective, there is always evolution, and you can choose to go with its flow or resist it.

That was deep. So back to emotions.

It's anyone's guess what intricate and ambitious plan your soul has for this lifetime, but your emotions can give you a cheeky peek into what your soul is doing in the here and now. Emotions are an energy frequency that you can use to tune into your soul's purpose—and, ultimately, your most tender truth. The higher the frequency of your emotion, the more aligned you are with your soul purpose. A high frequency emotion is one that feels good—peace, satisfaction, contentment, bliss, love, etc. A low frequency emotion feels bad—frustration, anger, resentment, disappointment, you know them all. Life is always easier when you're operating in alignment with your soul, and you'll know when you are because you'll feel good.

Emotions can also be influenced by what's going on in the physical body. Perhaps you feel negative because you didn't get enough sleep or you need to poop. You might feel particularly euphoric because you've taken some good drugs. Learning to tune into your soul through your emotions requires that you understand your body and tune into it. Both of these require introspection. The clues are on the inside, not the outside. Sit with yourself, focus inward, and observe without allowing your logical brain to interject with its opinions and distractions and judgey comments. Become familiar with the sensations that arise from within. Your logical mind will want to get in on the act to interpret them and assign meaning to them. The brain is prone to grabbing your emotions and analysing them to death, so you must loosen the brain's grip on your emotions during this process so that they can remain intact as they move through your body and back out again.

It can be a wobbly start, learning to trust your emotions. Even recognising them can be hard if you're not used to doing it. Emotions are like an interactive library with 24/7 access; just because you can't read yet, you shouldn't avoid wandering inside to have a look at what's there.

When your soul is in the driver's seat while your human is intent on adhering to routine, there can be conflict, times where your soul will be going one way and your human reckons they need to go the other. Your soul says, "All right, everyone! Rest stop. Everybody out. We are going to take a break." And your human responds, "What are you slowing down for? It's Wednesday, we've got a 9:00 a.m. meeting to get to. Speed up! Speed up!" Your soul is taking the foot off the accelerator, and your human is trying to floor it. Your soul isn't operating in isolation though. Your soul is the universe. You are the universe. Everything is connected, and everything is operating in perfect harmony. Except for your human. So when you tune into your soul, you're tuning into the entire flow of the universe. No matter what opinion that tiny, young, immature part of your brain has about how you should be doing Wednesday, the universe and your soul know better. And if your emotions are telling you that today you're going to slow down, then you've got two choices: You can slow down or you can have an uncomfortable Wednesday. You can argue with logic, but you can't argue with emotion. Emotion just is.

While I was learning this lesson, I had a lot of uncomfortable Wednesdays. The universe was putting its foot on the brakes, but my habit was to accelerate the hell out of there. So it took some serious courage to pay attention to my emotions and integrate them into my operating model. There were lots of times that I would turn up to work with an agenda and a plan, a tried and true methodology that I was going to adhere to. I had a workshop to run. I had points to make. I had coloured whiteboard pens. But my emotions said, "You don't feel like doing any of this. You just want to sit back and relax today." And I would yell back to them, "THERE IS NOTHING ABOUT THIS SCENARIO THAT IS REMOTELY RELATED TO EARNING A LIVING!" I even snidely added one time, "And how exactly do you think I'm going to run a workshop by doing fuck-all anyway?"

The universe answered. It gave me a migraine. I turned up to the workshop with my plan and my points and my whiteboard markers, and all I was capable of doing was handing the pens to another participant and asking them to describe what they thought the agenda should be while I slumped in a corner. Each person then took a pen and discussed with the group their understanding of what the issues were and how they might be solved. They collaborated in front of my very (sore) eyes. No surprises that it ended in classic rom-com style, where the team bonds and the client is happy and the mean boss has a change of heart and becomes everybody's best friend. Fade to black, credits roll superimposed with still pictures of the team backslapping, chugging beers at the pub afterward, and complex etchings on the whiteboard which are the future blueprint for peace on Earth and goodwill to all men. Upbeat music finally ends with a picture of me asleep in a chair as the cleaner turns out the conference room lights. I think I've milked that cliché as much as I can.

Universe knows best, and your emotions are tuned into it. Emotions are the guardrails reminding you when you're on track. And even when you're not on track, it's still all part of the grand plan. Contradictory? Yes. They're called divine contradictions. There will be many more throughout this journey. The universe is full of them. Just ask any quantum physicist.

CULTIVATING NEW FEELINGS

So you've serenaded your emotions one at a time and you have gotten to know each of them well. You're pretty sure you know which ones you like, which ones you never want to see again, and the ones you might be happy to follow on Instagram so that you don't have to engage them directly but who you can call on in the unlikely event you do need them. And then there is the final group: The handful of emotions that you are so madly in love with you never want them out of your sight.

When I first got up close and personal with my feelings, it was clear that I was hanging out with some pretty bad influences, and I had some work to do. In fact, there was one particular emotion I should have dumped years ago because he treated me so badly, and yet, inexplicably, he was still hanging around. Even when I wasn't with him, he was lurking on the sidelines, ready to leap forward and shit on everything I did.

He would turn up at any time. He would let himself into my place, leave his mess and his dirty footprints all over my stuff, and I was powerless to do anything about it. I'd be enjoying my day, and then suddenly, boom, he would turn up and everything would be pants.

Popular culture has it that if you feel bad, you should change something in your environment to feel better. You have to break up with somebody or get a new job or move interstate or buy a new house or grow out your hair or shave it all off. But in reality, it's the other way around. Learn to cultivate the emotion you want internally first, and then it will flavour everything external. It's also a lot cheaper than trying to control all those environmental variables, many of which are only semi-controllable.

Learning to do this is where the bad boyfriend analogy gets a bit dicey because the next step is not that you need to break up with him as much as you just need to start going out with someone else. It's a little bit controversial.

So if the emotions I don't want are the ones that leave a mess all over my house and a bad stink in the carpet, then the ones I do want are like having a party. But it's not one of those frenetic, death-by-small-talk parties where loud, obnoxious people get drunk and trash the place. This is an illumination party, outdoors, where the trees are decorated with fairy lights and there is a grove under the leafy canopy, which disappears into the semi-darkness and leads me deep into a forest. There are tiny candles on either side of a wooden path to guide me along the way. A fire pit burns with aromatic wood, and sparks from the flames fly up into the night, making me gaze toward the sky where I see three shooting stars. The grove opens into a clearing where a DJ mixes blissful grooves. And there's a sweet smell of incense in the air, which might be from the fire pit but might be from somewhere or someone else. I see you standing by the fire. The softest, warmest breeze rustles the tree leaves. This makes you look up, and when you do, you see a light show in the sky. You take off your shoes and stand in the grass. You are handed a drink, and I introduce you to your new soulmates, the other guests. It's all very chill. There's a flow to it. You sip from your stained-glass goblet as you wander down the embankment to a stream and wade into the water. The food served is infused with the divine, and it tastes so good that you feel like your mouth is expanding.

The next day, when the party's over, you keep getting happy reminders of the night before—the smell of woodsmoke in your hair, glitter between your toes, and, best of all, leftover cake neatly stacked in containers in the fridge.

Whoa. That was a trip. I feel like I've been sitting on public transport, day-dreaming about sex, and I've just snapped out of it. What was I saying? Oh yeah, cultivating good emotions. Here's a quickstart guide, and if you want more detail, head on over to kateangel.com where there's some fun stuff to get you there and keep you there.

While observing introspectively, identify all the different emotions you typically date. Now pick out the ones you'd prefer to feel (up. Ba-dum.). With this shortlist of preferred emotions, you're going to cultivate them one at a time to bring them to life in your body more and more often. Use your memory, your imagination, your storytelling skills, whatever you've got (even exploring the outer regions of truth and fiction) to pull yourself into the frequency of a given emotion to feel it as intensely as you can. Do this as often as you can. Even fifteen seconds while you're waiting in line at the meat counter is a great start. Recreate the awe you feel at a fireworks display, the bliss of a job well done, or the confidence of knowing what to do. Whatever emotion it is, repeat this little exercise often, and, eventually, you will convince your brain to use its autopilot feature. Then it will program that good feeling for you so that you don't have to invoke it manually. More and more, you will find yourself slipping into that feeling without choosing to do it, without even thinking about it, and without it being dependent on what's going on in your external environment. It will become a default.

Give it a whirl. Worst case, you'll have to endure fifteen seconds of bliss.

Before leaving the feeling department and heading to the next chapter, decide to tune into how you feel every chance you get by stopping what you are doing for a minute, focussing on your body, and allowing yourself to notice the feelings moving around inside. Invite your feelings in so they can become familiar rather than ostracising them and treating them like the enemy. Your feelings are like that nerdy kid from your neighbourhood who you've always ignored but who's been in love with you since kindergarten and who is about to become the good-looking hero that swoops in and saves you from certain death by inauthenticity.

CHAPTER 3

BELIEVE

WHERE DO BELIEFS COME FROM?

Beliefs are like food, and, typically, you only get to choose what you eat once you're old enough. When Nigel Newborn arrived, his community was already eating their Weet-Bix and their raspberry popsicles and their sardines on toast. Nigel doesn't even know what food is yet. He gets a plate put in front of him and a spoon, and he takes it at face value and in it goes. And typically, as a family, you all eat the same beliefs. You all sit down to the dinner of beliefs, and everyone unquestioningly ingests the beliefs, and the beliefs get assimilated into your body and become part of you. And so the way you use your energy and the way you operate now is based on a belief you ate at a meal years ago. That's how beliefs work.

Have you ever had fresh salmon in a restaurant done properly by the chef who knows how it should be done? Chargrilled on the outside, raw on the inside, succulent, dissolves in your mouth. It's absolutely delicious. Or so I've heard. I've never had it. I'm working on myself so that I can, but I've been trained to eat salmon that has been overcooked into orbit. My life experience generated a belief that salmon must be cooked all the way through before it can be safely eaten. This belief is now so deeply established that my body has developed habits and behaviours to support it; I get grossed out by the thought of putting uncooked salmon in my mouth. I can't bring my teeth to bite into the raw interior in case I gag and really expose myself.

Logic and the people around me say, "It's safe to eat rare salmon." And, of course, I can see evidence that this is true because they're putting rare salmon in their mouths and are ecstatic about it and not dropping dead. And while I agree with them from a rational standpoint, my body's reflexes simply won't respond to logic. This involuntary part of my body is not connected to my logic centre. It's connected to my autonomic nervous system, which is the conduit between my body and my cognitive reasoning. I have to retrain myself. I will show you how you can do this in a sec.

Beliefs can be created by familiarity. They may be nothing more than something you experience repeatedly. They needn't be something you have chosen or accepted. They are a function of the brain's programmable nature, something you have been exposed to so often that it has been coded into autopilot; something you barely know is there.

Beliefs can be formed by something you are told repeatedly, whether it be a regular observation of something that exists (or doesn't exist) in your environment, advertising, news articles, conversations between the people around you, and so on, all leading to millions of little beliefs that swim around in your complex being, from "Nobody walks around barefoot" to "Music won't earn you a living" to even one that profoundly impacted me as a teenager of the 1980s: "Redheads can't wear pink."

Occasionally you will come across beliefs that you didn't know you had. They're old, out-of-date beliefs that are still running silently in the background. They can be quite embarrassing, especially when somebody else points them out. Like when I was chatting with a friend who mentioned that their car mechanic was out of town and they couldn't get their car fixed. I asked, "When will he (the mechanic) be back?" to which my friend teased, "Are you assuming my mechanic is male?" Upon being outed, my initial reaction was, "Where the hell did that come from? That's not mine! I didn't put that there!"

The assumption I made revealed a belief that might have been relatively sound in 1925, but it certainly didn't match my values now. I didn't even realise it was still active until it slipped out and somebody else noticed it. And as with my salmon story, just because I no longer agree with a belief and have decided I don't want it anymore, that doesn't mean I can instantly jettison it. My body and my habits still remember it. My speech, my reactions, my reflexes are all going to take some tidying up. It will take time, effort, and some kind of priority on the to-do list, but it's definitely doable.

Beliefs are complicated beasts. You've got a lot of them, all born at different times by different parents. Not surprisingly, sometimes they just can't agree with one another. This clash of beliefs can yield some strange and inexplicable results.

Consider my ongoing salmon ordeal. The only reason my salmon belief is such a saga is because my belief that "salmon must be cooked all the way through" clashes with my belief that "I am a cultured person." In my eyes, "I am a cultured person" means embracing fine dining. It means not asking for salmon to be cooked all the way through because that would offend the chef and show me as an uncouth heathen. So when I'm offered salmon, instead of simply specifying how I want it cooked, I blush and stammer and start babbling about the one time my husband got sick from oily fish and how tofu is a better choice on a half moon anyway. It's just plain weird.

Back to the "beliefs are food" analogy. You might appreciate that next time you behave strangely, or even inappropriately, that maybe you are being faced with having to eat a belief that you've never tried before. Perhaps you've only been fed a diet of unhealthy beliefs, and you are slowly learning that there are more nutritious foods to be had. Or that the foods you're used to eating are being phased out because they're bad for the environment, but maybe you can't afford to change your belief diet right now. Maybe you don't know how. Maybe you're scared shitless that you'll freak out if you put something in your mouth that you aren't familiar with.

It's important to know that you are not your beliefs. And accepting yourself even with your weird and wonderful blended family of beliefs is accepting your current truth, and that's being authentic.

WHAT ARE BELIEFS FOR ANYWAY?

Beliefs are the framework you use to make sense of your surroundings. If feelings are how you experience the world, then beliefs are the interpretation of those experiences. Beliefs determine when and which feelings should be activated. Beliefs tell you whether what is happening to you and around you is good or bad and whether it's worthy of your attention.

If I've grown up with the belief that all pigeons are bastards, then when I go out into the world, I'm going to be wary of pigeons, pictures of pigeons, places where pigeons congregate. I might even become hypervigilant around any bird that looks like a bastard. Beliefs dictate how you think. Over time, they become connected with certain emotions so that anytime a belief is used to interpret an experience in the real world, its associated emotion will also be triggered.

I met an eleven-year-old who was very sensitive to anybody who implied he might not be doing something well. So when his mother said, "Sweetheart, when you stack the dishwasher, could you make sure you rinse things first because a few things in here haven't been rinsed properly," he fell to pieces. The extent of his reaction didn't seem to match the comment he was reacting to. When this was unpacked (the reaction, not the dishwasher), it became clear that in the past, certain family members got angry at him for not doing things right the first time, and he had become fearful of letting them down. The underlying belief he was holding on to was "When I am not doing something right, I've hurt the people around me."

Everyone has something, many things, that they're more sensitive to than is useful for them. You see the world according to your beliefs, and it feels one hundred percent convincing. Hell, if you're feeling all this emotion, it better bloody well be true, otherwise you're wasting all this valuable emotion on something that doesn't matter. So if somebody asks you to rinse the dishes better before stacking the dishwasher, and you think they are upset because of it, then their upset is your absolute truth. Note that again for emphasis: Their upset is *your* truth, not theirs.

By the time you're an adult, you've got so many beliefs vying for superiority and attention in your mind that, as you navigate your way through the world, it's hard telling which of them are influencing your reality to create a multicoloured truth mural that's exclusively yours but indiscernible to others. There are decades of history behind most of these beliefs, but because they are so familiar to you, you don't even recognise them as mere beliefs, so you conclude that what you experience must be the *truth*. And you're going to defend these beliefs as truth too because the possibility of them not being real is like being told: "Sorry, the world is in fact flat after all." Imagine what it would be like to receive convincing evidence that this belief, or any other major belief from which you have constructed your reality, wasn't true. You would feel like the ground beneath you was caving in. You would search through your memory for counterevidence and throw any logic at it that you could to try and explain it another way so that you could hold onto your belief. If that failed, denial would be your next strategy. Sound familiar? It's scary changing beliefs. What if everyone else still believes the old belief, and you're the only one who has realised it's not true? How about if the fallen belief is connected to other beliefs in a "If this is true, then this must also be true" kind of way; if one belief falls, so do all the others. That's a terrifying prospect. You have built your life upon your beliefs. The things you consider important, the way you relate to people, what you choose to do with your day—they're all based on beliefs. If too many beliefs fall, then, in many ways, you may feel like the "You that you know" ceases to exist. Spiritualist Ram Dass experienced the disappearance of his identity during an acid trip once, and he said it was scary as fuck. Even though he was still physically present, he didn't know who he was anymore. Imagine how you would react if you realised that every person on the planet could, instead of working, just have money deposited into their bank account regardless of what they did each day as long as they filled in a short form. You'd feel totally ripped off for having misspent more than half your life. You might also feel pretty stupid.

So, for this reason, people like their beliefs to be rock solid. It makes them feel safe. But it stands to reason that at any point in time, there are a whole bunch of beliefs that you hold that are completely false; you just don't know it. How much evidence would you need to be convinced that your beliefs are unfounded and give them up?

Probably a hell of a lot more evidence than it took for you to adopt them in the first place.

I estimate that a good ninety-five percent of the things I believe I haven't actually verified myself. Sure, I grew up on a diet of "the Earth is round," and I'm going to defend it with my life, but I've never actually seen it being round in my own bodily experience. I've seen the photos. I've been in an aeroplane and gone halfway around the world and back, but I was asleep for most of that time. They could have steered that plane anywhere while I was out. Did I really take off from Sydney airport and fly west and come back into Sydney airport from the east? Well, I'm going to save my conspiracy theories for matters closer to home, such as: Are vegetables really good for me? And just because science says that M&Ms shouldn't be eaten for dinner, I haven't read the research, so can I really put my hand on my heart and say that it's true?

Beliefs are like the walls you live within that keep you secure, but they can also keep you trapped. Sometimes you find yourself feeling claustrophobic living within these narrow confines, and this can play out in your life as feeling stuck and unable to figure out what you want. Or, perhaps you can ascertain what you want, but you're unable to work out how to get it. A lot of those belief walls were built when you were very small, when it was okay to live in a smaller place. But now that you're bigger, you need more room to move, more freedom. Your survival is no longer dependent on having somebody within arm's reach at all times. You're more capable and knowledgeable, and you don't have the safety needs that you did when you were four years old. Beliefs like "If I am left alone, I will die" are common childhood beliefs and are intended to ensure your survival when you are young. This childhood pattern is still active in many adults, limiting their independence and happiness by further layering on similar beliefs like "I must have a partner to be happy." Knocking down these walls takes strength and effort. "What's on the other side? Will I still be safe? Do I have what I need to exist on the other side?" There are a bunch of unknowns that have to be accepted if a wall is to be taken down because, for as long as the wall exists, you only ever know what's on one side.

You hold on to your beliefs to varying degrees, but they also hold on to you. Releasing this grip takes courage. But if you are brave enough to do it, that's where the real evolution starts. Next is an exercise to identify obsolete beliefs and replace them with something more constructive.

IDENTIFY BELIEFS THAT NO LONGER SERVE YOU

Beliefs are the source of all woes. If you're ever feeling unhappy, scared, angry, offended, annoyed, or even just dissatisfied or irritable, and you've eliminated the need to sleep, eat, drink, or poop, you can bet that your beliefs are involved. Identifying beliefs can take a bit of crafty hunting. Beliefs like to disguise themselves. They hide behind societal norms, people's stories, and even behind feelings. But if you like solving riddles, enjoy being the sleuth in a good detective story, or are even open to a burlesque strip show, then this next bit is for you.

As good as they are at blending into the background and going unnoticed, there is one place you will always find beliefs poking out: In the things that trigger you. Triggers are emotional reactions to situations, people, or words. These are the things that you complain about and whine about; the things that people do that drive you nuts and shit you to tears. Beliefs are also evident behind the word "should"—the things you feel you or other people "should" do or be.

I did this belief-identification exercise for the first time with two of my pet hates: Slow Drivers and People Who Talk Too Much in Meetings. They both ended up tracing to the same core belief. Here's how it went down.

When I am stuck behind somebody driving slowly or even somebody walking slowly, I get inordinately frustrated. It happens even if I'm not in a hurry to get anywhere. Now, it's easy to logically justify my irritation: "Everybody's in a rush these days. We're all trying to save time, and nobody likes being stuck on the road longer than they have to be. The driver should pull into the left lane and let me pass, and they're not, so it makes sense that I would be frustrated."

But that's all in my head. That's the rationale, the reflection back of what society's been telling me all this time. That's the first layer. The striptease begins when I take that layer off and look underneath at the feeling itself. I tap into the feeling I get when I am actually stuck in a car behind a slow driver. When I tell the story about the feeling rather than the story about how wronged I am, then it's something different altogether. This is the story where I've been accelerating, I'm going at a good pace, I'm getting where I need to go, I'm feeling free, making progress, and then, suddenly, boom, I have to put my foot on the brake. I have to slow to a snail's pace, which is excruciatingly slower than before. It's a feeling of urgency. It feels like there's not just somebody stuck in front of me but that something is behind me too, pushing me forward, and I'm trying to hold it back. I'm sandwiched between that pressure behind me and the obstruction in front of me, and I'm feeling responsible for both, like I need to solve this entire traffic jam on my own even though no traffic jam exists. There's a sense that I'm letting people down if I don't hurry up. That's the story about the feeling. And from that story, the beliefs that I am responsible for this problem and that I am letting people down are revealed.

Well, well, well, that's pretty different from thinking that the driver should just pull over to the left. That's a belief that goes way back. It predates this moment, this car trip; it predates my ability to drive.

For the first seven years of my life, I was the youngest child. Being younger, I was always slower than my older sibling and the adults in the family. I didn't know as much and wasn't as capable. It took me longer to do things, so I was always being rushed. I was the slowest eater in the world. I was always the last one left at the dinner table when everybody else was clearing up. In the morning, the entire family was ready to go except for me. So I believed, at that early age, that not only was I slow, but I was also preventing others from doing what they wanted to do. I was disappointing them. I was holding them back. Now being stuck behind slow drivers triggers the urgency feelings associated with the belief that I am slow, that I am not capable, that I am letting people down. And while there might have been a time many years ago where people were telling me I was slow, they're no longer telling me this anymore. They don't need to because I've taken over that role.

Likewise, it's no surprise that when I use the belief-identification technique to unpack a completely separate trigger—People Who Talk Too Much in Meetings—the not-serving-me belief turns out to be the same, even though the context and the logic underlying it are completely different. My logic is that these people are wasting taxpayer and shareholder money by not communicating effectively. The feeling I get is frustration—frustration that we're taking too long, that if I don't get clarity from this person soon, then I'll be in trouble by my bosses for not delivering. People will be *disappointed* and that, in turn, will *hold them back* from what they need to do. And, oh, hello! I'm back at the same place. All roads lead to the belief that I am disappointing others because I am slow. Who knew?

Annnnnd, I've created my very own riddle. What do people who talk too much in meetings and slow drivers have in common?

The emotional reaction you have to many things in life is often not commensurate with the momentary event that causes it. People all have different beliefs and, therefore, different triggers. It can even be triggering when other people don't share your triggers. They might look at you and say, "What's the big deal? Calm the fuck down!" and all the things that just serve to make you feel worse. Note to self, there's another trigger: Getting Told to Chill Out When I'm Feeling Uptight. But those triggering situations you hate so much are actually incredibly valuable. They contain all sorts of useful nuggets to help you shift the negative emotions that hold you hostage to the whim of external events.

And no, you don't *have* to feel bad. While negative feelings can alert you to something happening in your environment that you need to pay attention to, you are under no obligation to feel prolonged negative emotion as a result of it. When you have been wronged, violated, or when you see something that is unjust, you often believe that feeling bad is how you honour the injustice. It is how you demonstrate to yourself and others what your beliefs are. But it is entirely possible to accept an injustice without succumbing to continued unhappiness. It won't diminish your belief in what's right and what's wrong.

While you let a bad thing ruin a good day, you rarely let a good thing ruin a bad day. You wind up just feeling bad more than you would like to, instead of saying to the universe, "Thanks for drawing this to my attention. I will now take appropriate action and put it behind me as quickly as possible." But maybe without being so formal.

In fact, when you are feeling like crap, you make worse decisions and take less appropriate action than if you were on an even keel, like yelling at a coworker who mouth-breathes too loudly instead of calmly relocating yourself.

Because beliefs and feelings form so much of your sense of identity, understanding them is essential to discovering your truth. Using triggers to explore your feelings and understand the beliefs that root them is how you take back your power. Self-discovery and insight will lead you to the realisation that you are not at the mercy of a disordered universe and everyone and everything in it. You have the authority to choose not just your feelings but also your beliefs, and from this place, beautiful things will sprout.

If you want to do this as a guided exercise for yourself, head over to my website at kateangel.com where you'll find an exercise that walks you through it step by step. Take the exercise slowly. Some of those beliefs are so firmly ingrained that dislodging them can feel very uncomfortable at first. If you move too fast, they'll get even more resistant. And if you have trauma from the past or things get too unpleasant, don't be discouraged; this is an opportunity to find professional help so you don't have to go the rest of the way alone.

YOUR REALITY

Let's just get this straight: Your feelings are your reality, and you now know how to cultivate whichever ones you want to feel. Beliefs are the soil from which your feelings sprout and you can choose which of those you want to plant in your life. So if that's the case, then reality is whatever you want it to be. Suddenly life has exploded into another dimension. The world has become soft and malleable like fresh Play-Doh that you can mould to your liking rather than the immovable and incomprehensible Stonehenge you always thought it was.

So what are you waiting for? I'm not waiting for anything; I've already left. I've called in the construction crew. I'm going to build myself a castle from naturally grown hemp and plant palm trees and wear ancient Egyptian bling from the Louvre and barbeque free-range organic food that has been grown in my very own veggie garden tended by horticulturalists who dress in earthy tones and love what they do. I'm going to escape the tiny space of beliefs I'm living in. I don't even need the demolition team for that. I just need to push my way through a hedge and streak down the hill in my pyjamas toward a beautiful meadow of my own creation in which my new reality awaits.

Investigate your feelings and your beliefs often, and you'll eventually uncover the tiny house of beliefs that you currently inhabit. It's an archeological dig where you're exposing a little wall here and an outhouse there. You're one of those first intrepid explorers who set off hundreds of years ago to map the planet with no clue about what land masses might be found. Soon you'll realise, "Oh my God, I'm living in a cramped little humpy with low ceilings!" You'll realise how small your world is and how much you've fenced yourself in. And that's when you can play a real live version of an escape room. It's one big game of Get the Fuck Out.

YOUR INTEGRITY

The reality where you are feeling the feelings you want to feel and believing the beliefs you choose to believe feels a lot more like your authentic self. And you know that this is entirely possible. You'll also know when you're on track because if it feels good, then it's aligned. You're still living in the physical world because you can still apply logic to discern the consequences of the decisions you make. The real-world consequences of wearing socks with thongs in public or yelling at somebody instead of having a civilised conversation haven't gone away, but you will be able to make decisions from a place of empowerment and balance rather than a place you haven't chosen to be.

And now a quick broadcast from the overprotective ego: "But if we all do what we want then there will be chaos." Unless you're concerned that you are one of those people who will start looting and murdering people once you give yourself permission to be yourself, then my advice is to not worry about it. You're protected by your own feelings. The thing that stops most people from committing heinous crimes is that you just don't want to. You really don't feel like it. I'm convinced that if people were living in alignment with their souls, there'd be a lot less mayhem, not more. When people accept their authentic selves, there is less angst.

Remember the pain you experience when you don't allow yourself to feel your primary emotions and instead start having opinions about how bad they are? That pain goes away when you accept yourself and acknowledge your feelings as your authentic self. Emotional pain, including all the unconscious beliefs and buried feelings from the past, makes people do terrible things, awkward things, and counterproductive things. Have a look at your own most badly-behaved moments and see what emotional place you were in at the time that fuelled your actions. As you become aware of these hidden motives and start to change them, your actions will become more conscious, and you will leave way less destruction in your wake. You will become so much happier.

With practice and observation, you'll get better at knowing when you're in your truth or if you're lying to yourself. Because no matter how good the logic of what you're saying or thinking sounds, your body knows the truth, and when you stop long enough to pay attention to it, you can feel it. But even more difficult than dealing with your own lies is living your truth in the face of other people who think that you're not being honest. Have you ever been in a situation where you share something about yourself and people stare back at you like you're crazy? Or they loudly proclaim "That's bullshit!" It's hard to not back down. It takes strength and courage to not doubt yourself and wonder if maybe you got it wrong, that it was a dumb idea after all, or that you don't belong. Think about that one for a minute because that's what this life is all about. It's about learning how to identify your genuine truth, knowing within yourself what that is, and standing steadily beside yourself in an act of self-love, recognition, and solidarity as your actions and choices reflect that truth, even when others are watching.

Consider this a tip to help you stay on track with your evolution: If feelings and beliefs create one's reality, and your different experiences have created feelings and beliefs that are unique to you, then it follows that everyone's living in a different reality. So, of course, people won't get you, not fully. And you will never entirely get them. That's one more reason to live authentically—you might as well. You can finally stop feeling bad when you don't understand people, when you feel like you don't get it, or you don't have the answers. And you can let go of expecting people to get you.

CHAPTER 4

INTERPRET

When I was little, my older brother used to say to me, "Hey Kate, what does Kate mean?" He would then watch my seven-year-old mind flail with this existential problem. This chapter is about the meaning you assign to the things in your life. Your life experiences are not what define you; rather, it's how you interpret those experiences.

STORYTELLING

While I was at university, one of my psychology lecturers told the class a story. She was on a train when a father with three children got on. The man sat down while the kids ran about the carriage yelling and screaming—they were swinging around the poles, falling over and hurting themselves, and arguing with one another. The man, meanwhile, sat on his own as if they didn't even exist. My lecturer observed the other passengers getting more and more agitated at the children's behaviour and at the father's complete lack of interest in them. The other passengers were watching each other almost as if to see who would be the first to get up and tell this guy to look after his children. When one of the children fell face-first into another passenger, that passenger finally stood up and went over to the man. At this point, everybody was unobtrusively looking/not looking to see what would happen next.

"Mate," the passenger said to the father, "do something about your kids, they're going feral."

At which point, the father looked up as if noticing for the first time he was in a train and said, "I'm so sorry. We've been at the hospital where their mother just died and I don't even know what I'm meant to be doing."

Everything shifts with reframing. I've long since forgotten the point my lecturer was making by telling the story, but my point is this: You will never know somebody's full story. And just as with beliefs and feelings, you often don't know your own. Everyone has hidden motivations and drivers, so when you make up somebody else's story for them, and then proceed to believe it, you're travelling somewhat precariously, making loads of assumptions. That same psychology lecturer said that humans by nature make up stories to fill in the blanks.

When it comes to the things you can't verify or don't seem to make sense, then give people the benefit of the doubt. Craft a background story that makes you feel good, not bad. Positive feelings make you focus on opportunities and are more likely to be associated with gratitude, constructive thinking, and creativity. Negative feelings make you focus on threats and cynicism, which are more likely to be associated with a scarcity mindset and emotional instability. Start with yourself. You can take any story of your own life and reframe it to something equally as true, just better. You do this inadvertently all the time with your memories. If you are in a good mood when you remember something from the past, you are more likely to describe the memory in positive terms. When you are in a bad mood, the memory is painted with a darker brush. You use your memories as ammunition to fuel your negativity, to keep yourself feeling shitty. And that's just downright mean.

Stories are how human beings make sense of the world. Even though what you are describing is often too complex to make full sense of it all, you do it anyway because it's the only mechanism you have to keep yourself moving forward. You are bombarded by hundreds of bits of information via your senses everyday, and storytelling is the simplest way your brain can observe it all, construct a narrative, and process it without expending too much energy. Narratives can be powerful, so learning to consciously employ the storytelling tool with the right intentions to tell a story about the best version of yourself is a game changer.

Case in point: About four or five years ago, my husband, a drummer, got together with a guitarist and a singer to jam in our back shed. But the one thing they were missing was a bass player, so I offered to be the missing piece. I dusted off a few rudimentary guitar-playing skills from childhood, bought a second-hand bass guitar, and joined in. It was more fun than I could ever have imagined. I wanted to become an amazing bass player so I could have even more fun, but I wasn't improving fast enough, and, therefore, I got frustrated very quickly. This new mindset flavoured how I saw the whole experience. It drew my focus to my inadequacies instead of the fun that it was possible to have, and, suddenly, I wasn't enjoying myself anymore. When people found out we were playing music and asked if we were any good, the best I could muster was, "Depends if you're asking Bono or my mum."

Meanwhile, the rest of the group was having heaps of fun. A violinist joined us, and she started having fun. The neighbours over the back fence who could hear us playing the oldies and the goodies also found it fun. There was a parallel story playing out, which was just as available to me: My friends didn't give a shit how bad I was because we were still having heaps of fun. They were completely accepting of my level of ability. And in reality, who knows? They might not have been any better than me, but I was so focussed on myself that I didn't notice.

All it took to get myself back into the groove was to change the words I used, shifting the narrative and the story. Now I say things like, "I'm living proof of just how much you can rock out at beginner level" and "I'm in a band." Nowadays, if you were to ask me if we are any good, I would probably stare at you uncomprehendingly and then ask you to reframe the question to "Are you having fun?"

Tastes so much better, yes?

Take a look at some of the stories that have been told to you, and question whether they are helping you be the highest version of yourself or whether they are stifling your authenticity. This helped me to learn that the stories in the Bible are just metaphors. God isn't necessarily a thinking, opinionated entity that makes decisions about your fate. There isn't actually a fire beneath you being stoked in readiness for the day you've been too naughty to ever recover, it's just a way of helping human beings understand that which actually is beyond comprehension—just like the made-up stories about the day-to-day experience of being human. There is no absolute truth when it comes to describing feelings and life's most important concepts. Once I realised this, the nonsensical suddenly made a lot more sense, and I was free to describe things on my terms without worrying that I was being a liar. I could now branch out of my limited thinking and explore the possibility that God could be a feeling, not a person, and hell could be a state of mind, not a physical place. In the past, I've shared this with people who tell me sympathetically that they had all this figured out by the time they finished high school. But their eye-rolling didn't diminish the beautiful feeling of release and expansiveness it had on me even though I was forty-five years old. It was like I was soaring past my own limitations into a delicious new reality. These lessons can come at any time.

All that took me in the direction of discovering my authentic self. Uncertainty and ambiguity about the truth became very useful. Before this, my need to be seen as polite and telling the truth had always held me back for fear that I would get the truth wrong. As a result, I was always trying to describe this nebulous truth in terms of what I thought other people thought it was. I stifled my own learning and stopped asking questions because I was scared my ideas about how the world did or could work would be misunderstood and cause me to be rejected. And then, I even started to question my own integrity because I couldn't calibrate myself against the movable feast that was other people's opinions. But now I realise that all I was doing was holding out on myself and ignoring my own truth. My own truth is like a gift that I can take advantage of—it's mine to explore. As a result, the world has suddenly expanded tenfold. By learning how to reframe your understanding of your world, you expand it. It gives you the freedom to explore, and it gives you more to explore. And that, my scrumptious humans, is like getting access to an enormous theme park instead of a set of swings and a seesaw. The more there is to explore, the richer the opportunities you have to discover yourself. So awesome.

REWRITE THE FAIRY TALES

At the beginning of my own safari through the self-awareness wilderness, a colleague lent me a book she thought I might like. She'd put it in a brown paper bag, and I had waited until I got home before

I looked inside. The first thing I noticed was the title, which had the word "God" in it. "Well, I won't be reading *that*," I thought.

I gave religion my best shot in high school when it was all moaned-out hymns, weekly 1980s-style religious education, and chapel every Tuesday where the minister wouldn't let us make song requests. The way it was explained to me didn't make any sense, and I didn't get how some people loved it so much. So Christianity and I decided to amicably walk away from each other with the agreement that if we met each other on the street, we would look the other way.

Some months after I had been lent the book, after the requisite amount of time had passed to pretend like I'd actually read it, I picked it up so I could return it. I was on my way out the front door, book in hand, when something nudged me to open it. Within the first couple of lines, I was so engrossed in the pages that I literally sat down right in the hallway, not even making it to the couch, and devoured it in a reading frenzy.

The book was *Conversations with God* by Neale Donald Walsch, and it is definitely not a book about religion. In fact, Christianity only features when Neale offers some constructive feedback on how some of the concepts in the Bible really could be quite useful if they were only better presented, and that perhaps the church might consider modernising and reframing it to get the most out of those elusive little nuggets.

But do you know what I loved most about Walsch? It was the way he drew an empowering picture of humans and their ability to build a beautiful future existence where they have enough of their shit together to make the most of all the good stuff on offer. It's that same stuff that, right now, you are likely ignoring because you're too busy fixating on the scarcity in your life. It was like a fairy tale, and it was so different to the one I was living.

The fairy tales I'd heard as a child were similar to the *Barbie* movie. They were about the little princess who is told that when she grows up she can do anything she wants, but, most likely, she'll want to go to university. This is because she is smart, and that's what smart girls like to do. She can study anything she wants because she has choices, lots of choices, so isn't she so, so very lucky?

Then, when she's finished university, she can get a job, any job she wants because she is so clever, and the world is full of opportunities for clever, university-educated women such as her.

Then, and preferably only then, the girl gets to hook up with a prince or another princess for good. Maybe even both, but only one at a time because that's how things are done. Then, once she has met enough royalty, she gets to pick her favourite and take him or her home for keeps.

Then the dream couple can have kids. They can do those things, and they can also add a mortgage to their list of accolades because the bank will lend them money. The bank wants to lend them money because she is earning a lot of it, so getting the mortgage is a very good thing. And they live happily ever after.

And that's it. Lights come back on. Mind the step on your way out. I was in my late forties and had done all the "right" things, but I was a bit sketchy on how the "happily ever after" bit worked. Was there a sequel or something? It seemed a bit premature to be finishing the journey and resting on my laurels.

Part of my own awakening involved understanding that the first fairy tale was never intended to be an ongoing series. It was Walsch who made me realise that you have to write your own Season Two. Nobody is going to give it to you, and after having spent the first forty years of my life living society's prefab version of a fairy tale, I realised that's not what I wanted anyway. I wanted to be living my own story. It's a daunting but exciting task, writing your own story, but this discovery expedition you're on is about doing exactly that. The belief and feelings investigations that you did in Chapters 2 and 3, as well as your flourishing storytelling skills and the power of your imagination—all of which will strengthen in subsequent chapters—are the tools you need to start building your own story, *Fairy Tale: The Sequel.*

Is there a common story you buy into that wasn't written by you? How has this framed your expectations of how your life should or could be? And where has it limited you or empowered you?

THE PRECARIOUS ACT OF SPEECH

Unless I'm in a musical or interpretive dance kind of a space, my stories and fairy tales always involve words, and the way people use words just happens to be one of my favourite topics to poke fun at because language is so gloriously inadequate for anything important. Unless you are reading a recipe or giving someone directions in the street, use of language comes with some serious side effects. For all the meaningful things in my life, I've come to the conclusion that the true purpose of language is to show me how much more evolved I have yet to become. It's a true test of the human spirit.

When I was a teenager, I asked a friend one afternoon if she would like to come to my house and hang out. She said, "I'm tired. I think I'll go home." Those are the exact words she used. But when those same words reached my brain, I heard, "I don't like you anymore."

Isn't that amazing? How the words can come out with one intention, momentarily float through the air, and then get received by the other person with a completely different intention?

It's like a magic trick where you as the audience are left wondering, "How did you DO that?"

Words are the best argument starters. Even though most of the time people usually mean the same thing, just expressed in different words, this never fails to get things heated. My family is exceptional at pointing out when an inappropriate word has been used.

"Look at the gorgeous flowers on that tree over there!" somebody might say.

And the reply will be, "It's not a tree, it's a bush!"

Missed the point completely. Conversation derailed. Shared moment of beauty missed.

I have endless amounts of compassion for people who make the wrong word choices when they're talking. I've messed up my own word choices way too many times in my life not to.

I was taught very young that you needed to be polite to people, and one of the ways you did this was by using nice words to reflect the kindness you felt toward them.

I put this into practice when I was in kindergarten. My best friend's sister, who was only about three or four years old at the time, had had an operation on her eye. She was just out of hospital and was still feeling pretty sorry for herself.

So I wandered up to her thinking, "I can help here. I know what to do." I knew that she was probably feeling quite self-conscious about the look of her eye while it was healing, and I wanted her to know that I wasn't going to be one of the people who would rudely point and stare. So I walked up to her while she was standing next to her mother and I said, "Hi, Ally, your eye is so disgusting, I can't look at you."

And to me that reflected everything I wanted to say. It reflected the tone of compassion. It also indicated that I wasn't going to be staring at her. In short, I felt I had nailed it.

So . . . I know what it's like when you talk with one intention and it gets interpreted completely differently.

Truly, the spoken word is a battlefront. Just by walking out your front door and opening your mouth in front of people, you are engaging in a huge act of courage and bravery. You should be commended. Speaking is not for the faint-hearted. Maybe that's why babies don't come out of the womb already talking. Because they know what I'm talking about. And you know what they say about babies—that they are born with all this otherworldly wisdom, which they then lose, and there's nothing better than learning language to really speed up that transition. You lose that free-form experience of the world as you learn to define things with words.

Words play a crucial role in shaping your self-awareness and perception. Just like your beliefs, words narrow your view of the world and force you to see things in a particular way. Just look at the word "happy." Does it really describe everything that's going on for you when you use it to describe yourself? And is it the same feeling for you right now as it was last month when you also used that word? Squeezing an experience into a word or phrase is like shoving an entire slice of pizza into your mouth—it's rarely a perfect fit and you lose bits in the process.

If you're like me, and you're not interested in taking a vow of silence to avoid the pitfalls of language, then speech becomes yet another opportunity for growth and discovery. Authenticity means aligning your words, your actions, your thoughts, and your feelings so that they all reflect each other and follow the same intent. That starts with no longer using words to lie to yourself. The words you use can significantly influence your ability to be honest with yourself about who you are and how you show up in the world. Words make you vulnerable—and, in many cases, the words you say out loud can be weaponised and used against you down the line. But making the decision to live in your truth includes consciously choosing the words that reflect your truth even if those words are in opposition to all the words around you. Choosing words that speak your truth, but that are also compassionate toward yourself and your audience, is like having two balls in the air at all times. It's a skill that takes practice. So, starting from now, I encourage you to observe your word choices without judgement and to do the same when listening to others. Awareness alone can bring about truly significant change for the better.

You can be mindful of how the language you use makes you feel, and, in doing so, you can also arm yourself against other people's word choices. Consider these familiar childhood favourites. Remember accusing someone—or being accused—of something like "You're in love with yourself" or "You think the sun shines out of your own arse"? Aren't these things people actually *want* in their lives? Surely self-love and light shining from every part of you, not just your bum, is what everyone is aspiring for? Imagine yourself as a kid having one of these terms thrown at you by the schoolyard bully, and instead of crying and running away in shame, you break into a big smile and say, "Yeah, thanks, Bruce. My mum said so too," and then skipping off joyously to play on the swings.

Whether you're having a good day or a bad day, your reaction to other people's words is a mirror that reflects your own feelings. If somebody's words are making you feel bad about yourself, then they've just poked at one of your beliefs. You can then say (just to yourself, probably), "Oh, look, there's a belief I can throw away. Where's the toilet? I'll chuck it in there right now and flush it away forever."

Keep that symbolic toilet with you at all times so that you can clean up as you go and not have to wait until you get home. Just because someone has said something to you or about you, it doesn't mean it's true. If it feels true, explore the beliefs you have associated with this truth. If you flush as you go, you maintain your power and your energy in the moment because nobody likes having to hold it in when they really need to go.

So anytime you see or hear something said by someone else, and you find yourself feeling judged, just get a metaphorical flush going and spray a little air freshener. Flush, fresh, and huzzah!

And while I'm on a roll with the toilet analogy, sometimes your mental sewerage system can't cope with all the stuff you put down the toilet. Here is an opportunity for somebody to help you unblock your toilet. You've made a big mess in the bathroom and you've been too embarrassed to tell anybody about it because you're so ashamed. Keeping all of this to yourself has caused tremendous discomfort and grief. So you've been making do with this hideous toilet that you can't share with anyone. If somebody needs a toilet, you definitely don't want them to use yours. So you've been hiding it, and it's been traumatic. And then suddenly you find somebody who says, "Oh, trauma toilet? Yeah, I know all about that. That's my specialty. I can help you with your toilet." And that's what a therapist is, or any safe person who can listen without judgement. Sometimes you have a mess that requires more than one person to sort out. Find someone to unblock the toilet with you. Seriously, they can help you unblock that toilet, and they actually like it. They can show you how the toilet is unblocked. If you get a good toilet specialist, they can show you how to install a self-cleaning toilet so that you'll never have to deal with that big mess that you made in the toilet all those years ago, ever again.

Using your words to express your trauma and your experiences allows you to process what has happened to you and to make sense of it. In order to heal and move into more advanced stages of self-discovery, it is necessary for you to integrate your experiences into your sense of self, your identity, rather than reject them. Trauma causes a disconnection from the self as the brain wants to protect itself from the pain. In essence, your brain treats the trauma as though it has happened to someone else, which allows you to cope with the overwhelm of the experience. Using your words gives language to your experiences and connects you with the trauma, allowing you to start to accept that it has happened. While it might seem counterintuitive to connect with trauma, integrating the experience into your identity is necessary to heal the fractured parts of yourself, which inadvertently allows you to show up in the world as a whole person. This is the power of words in your own life and in the discovery of your authentic self. Making a decision to talk about what has happened to you, and making a decision to disempower the trauma and the negative beliefs you adopted as a result of the trauma, allows you to move through the pain and make decisions from a place of awareness. Language brings life.

FEMININE AND MASCULINE ENERGY

Whenever I started a new government contract, a friend of mine used to call me to say, "Whatever you do, don't be yourself." And we used to laugh hard because we've always joked about how I was the unlikeliest person to be working in a government office. I had been playing that unlikely role in the government sector for over two decades, sacrificing my true self in order to fit in. I used to think it was just me, until I started hearing similar stories from women from all walks of life, in all types of industries. I found this both fascinating and disturbing. I thought I'd take a closer look, and I noticed one thing in particular that people do to fit in at work, and how this can profoundly influence their alignment with their natural, balanced, authentic selves.

It started in the hot tub with my friend Alex. She told me what she'd had to do to become a partner of a large insurance firm in only two years. Essentially, she said she'd had to learn how to hustle and negotiate and push and shove and argue and to "keep up with the boys." She didn't say as much, but she gave the impression she can hail a taxi with a really good wolf-whistle. What she was describing to me sounded like a classic masculine stereotype from all those movies about Wall Street, where the male protagonist and his mates are boisterous, overassertive types who thrive in high pressure, chaotic environments. When I pointed this out to Alex, she agreed. In order to succeed at work, she'd had to behave like every cliché of a corporate man, and her femininity had taken a real hit as a result.

This nailed it for me. I felt exactly the same as Alex. And, as it turns out, so do many others (women, in particular) with whom I've spoken, in and out of the hot tub. Doing the next task or achieving the next big thing or delivering, planning, and executing or thinking and applying logic—all to achieve a result—are goal-oriented actions. This is the predominant focus of the working world, and it is how society measures productivity and success. These qualities, which allow you to take action, to move forward, and to deliver physical outcomes, are known as "masculine energy." Masculine energy is all about moving forward, and it's very much based in the material, physical world.

By contrast, feminine energy is about being. It's where you create. It's where you use your intuition. It's very much about listening, observing, feeling, and receiving. Time does not exist in feminine energy; there are no goals and no deadlines.

It's a pity these two modes of operating use the terms "masculine" and "feminine" because they're not about gender, they are about opposites. It would be better if they were called "light" and "dark" or "up" and "down" or anything other than words that connote men and women.

Both masculine and feminine energies are necessary for success as an individual and as part of the collective. Masculine and feminine energy influence and support each other in a feedback loop, and both are required for a balanced life.

Everybody has a balance of these two energies that is natural and unique for them, but when you're operating out of alignment with your natural balance, it starts to feel uncomfortable. Each moment requires a different blend of energies, but what is natural for you in that moment is unique to you. If your natural balance is to use your intuition to solve problems and you choose to ignore your intuition and use a quadratic equation instead, you will feel the pull to cross-check the mathematical answers with your intuition. If you ignore this pull, you will feel out of whack, a sense of unease, a feeling of dissatisfaction or frustration. If the equation and your intuition supply contradictory evidence, it'll feel even more painful. And exhausting.

How might your interpretation of yourself and your life be reframed in the light of how you balance your masculine and feminine energies? Could some of the issues you have, things you complain about, or your perceived lack of success be a result of an energetic imbalance?

There is a lot of good information out there on masculine and feminine energies. What I have included here will get you started on understanding the basic qualities that encompass each. Use this to observe your own balance. How often are you out of alignment? Learn to recognise how this feels as a way of getting to know yourself better and see how much more peaceful it is accepting your natural balance and working with it instead of against it. I found myself having less neck stiffness and eye strain after learning my true balance. Go figure, but I'm not complaining.

You can see how a clash can occur between your perception of the standard way to operate in a traditional work environment and the feminine-energy elements. And as I discovered in the bus queue one time while talking to a young student, it's not just the office where that's the case, it's in traditionally "feminine" roles like nursing too. This student told me how disempowering it felt that a caring, human-centred role had to be defined in such measurable, quantifiable terms. She had had to compromise on the connection she developed with the patients in order to meet her performance indicators, and it didn't feel right. She felt it was dulling her natural urge to nurture. Anywhere there is an imbalance of energy and rigid roles are in place, there will be disconnection from authenticity.

It is obvious to me that so many people are out of balance and have lost touch with feminine energy. I didn't even want to think about it too much because I was so proud of what I'd been able to achieve in the masculine, eye strain and neck pain aside. But once I observed this in my own life, I couldn't unsee it. This was an important contribution to my learning to integrate my authentic self back into society. I started to see the imbalance in energy in my work environment and where the lack of feminine energy was obstructing success. The traditional focus on doing, dollar values, analysing, metric-driven outcomes, and more doing meant little attention was given to intuition, creativity, flexibility, and a sense of natural flow. When the project team were feeling out of balance—frustrated, overworked, ignored, under-acknowledged, disrespected—there was no maturity in the project framework to acknowledge these states and how critical they were to the actual solution the team was seeking. I felt as if we were overlooking a large part of what we all had to offer. All this was painfully obvious to me, and yet I was the only one who could see it. Any attempt to talk about it was met with looks of utter confusion or pity—or even that expression people get when they've just figured out you're on hallucinogens. You can see why. Feminine energy is a relatively foreign concept because, for so long, anything to do with the feminine has been dismissed and criticised as weak, especially in a government office. So to avoid completely isolating myself from my colleagues, I kept quiet and instead started dreaming about what it would be like to live in a world where feminine energy was more valued.

I wake up in the morning and since it is a workday, the first thing I do is hop in an ocean rock pool for a nice, refreshing cleanse of the soul, and then I go for a walk in the forest because I need to absorb the wisdom from the trees. I need to embed myself in nature and observe the majesty around me, aligning my energy for the day so that by the time I leave the forest and get to work, I am oriented and ready to create beautiful things.

On arrival at work, I sit down with my colleagues and have a cleansing herbal beverage or a robust cup of Turkish coffee. We feel alive and beautiful and set our intentions for the day.

Today we are going to design a software application to allow schools and universities to submit their enrolment data to the government so that they can get the financial love that they need from this year's budget, and also so that the government can feel love for the education sector and do the right thing for them—and this will be easy because the information they receive is full of love and submitted with love. The data is just an embodiment of love.

My colleagues and I know that this is the vibe we want to influence what we are about to build. We want the educational institutions to feel unconditional love from the government so that every time they submit their data, they are offering it with reciprocated love through our excellent software solution, which is also the foundation of love upon which we will all grow and connect. And, as government, we also want to feel so much love toward these institutions because we're the Australian government and we're here to serve, and together, with this outstanding business solution, the consciousness of the Australian public and humanity in general will be levelled up. And indirectly, this loving vibe will also help calm down the tensions between Russia and Ukraine.

So we all sit down and hold hands and really get into that loving space because if anyone's slightly off that frequency, we're going to have problems and we're not going to get what we need—and we all remember stories from our childhood about the days when there was no love in government and, as a result, some really mongrel software solutions were released into the public domain with some particularly distasteful results.

We all sit there and we're cultivating that culture and, oh, wait, Malcolm. Malcolm's struggling.

Malcolm says sorry, his kids were wigging out this morning and he got stuck in traffic on the way to work and he didn't get that swim or the walk in the forest. And we say, with love, "It's okay, Malcolm. Take as long as you need because we all know how important it is for our lead solution architect to be feeling the love before we get started. So if you're not there, that's okay. We'll get you there."

Then Malcolm says, "Yeah, but you know what, though? It's really triggering me, the fact that you guys are there and I'm not."

That's when Siobahn says, "I know what you need. You need the bubble bath room. That's what you need. Maybe you need to go to the bubble bath room, sort yourself out, and we can wait. We can work on something else while you're gone. That's okay."

Malcolm's still not convinced.

Siobahn admits that it's probably she who needs the bubble bath, not Malcolm, because she should have had a herbal tea this morning instead of the Turkish extra strength.

Malcolm says, "I think I need the scream room. I need to go throw an axe. I need to smash something. And then when I come back, I'm going to be feeling good."

Yay! And suddenly we have our schedule for the morning. Those of us who are feeling the love are going to work on something different, and we will all reconvene when Siobahn's had her rose-scented bubble bath and Malcolm's thrown an axe and everyone's in the frequency to work on the software development for the data submission for educational institutions.

And, as it turns out, while Malcolm's in the scream room and Siobahn's in the bath, they both come up with some amazing ideas as they transition from their state of lack to their state of abundance, which they then bring back to the team to share. And the team meanwhile has also come up with some amazing concepts for the marketing and the communication strategy. And poof! Would you believe, lock and key, they all align perfectly. Suddenly so much work has been done even though we didn't plan for any of it. That's the feminine-energy office.

And, yes, this is an exaggeration, but I'm convinced that if there was a better balance between masculine and feminine energies in the workplace, then what I just wrote wouldn't seem at all far-fetched, perhaps just a little bit clichéd on account of the reference to herbal tea.

TRUTH, MASKS, AND SAYING IT LIKE IT IS

So, back in reality, I'm thinking about this guy I once worked with called Dean; he was the funniest person in the whole wide world. I used to set up a meeting and invite Dean, just so he could make me pee in my pantsuit. I don't actually know if we ever delivered anything or achieved what we were meant to, but it didn't matter. It was worth it. One day in one such meeting (I never liked that pantsuit anyway), Dean told us that he was so used to putting on his performing face that he had no idea who he really was underneath or whether there even was anybody underneath. He was saying it as a joke, but it really struck a chord with me, and I've thought about that moment ever since.

Dean is like so many people who have lost touch with their feminine energy in particular, and with themselves in general. They spend so long playing a role, pretending to be somebody else, that they forget who they really are. I have spent most of my life playing the comedian, hustling for laughs, just like I am doing right now, and I do it so that nobody sees the intense, serious person underneath because at some point in the past, I became ashamed of her. My fear was that when I really dug deep—delving beyond the masks layered on top of masks—I would no longer be able to relate to the stranger beneath or that I would find nobody under there at all. An even bigger fear was that I couldn t get naked even if I wanted to because those masks felt like they had melted onto my skin, and no amount of paint stripper was going to peel them off.

Let's just talk about honesty for a second and what it actually means when you're asked to tell the truth about yourself. I've always had a problem when watching those courtroom shows on TV where somebody is sworn to tell the truth, the whole truth, and nothing but the truth. I think, well, for starters, how long have you got? Because the whole truth is *everything I know*, and nothing but the truth is still everything just using different words. I could go on forever trying to satisfy those simple criteria because everything I know is linked to everything else, and there's always more I can tell you about something. Omit a single detail and I'm in big trouble for being a liar. So what is expected when someone is asked for the truth? And why does the truth make everyone feel so vulnerable?

And then there's that little issue of trust. I don't think I trust many people with the truth. I don't think I can trust them to handle the truth, and I can't necessarily trust them to know what my vulnerabilities are and then not use them against me. I have also come to realise that part of this issue with telling the truth is other people's reactions to the truth. Seeing how someone responds to your vulnerability can be unsettling. And putting yourself in a position to be seen for all you are is not an easy ask. But starting to observe means starting to expose your masks; it means starting to take risks. At the end of the day, honesty is the greatest risk of all. I was once applying for a security clearance, one of those really high-level clearances for working in government where they ask you all those confronting questions to see if they can find your vulnerabilities, such as how often you have sex with anybody or anything. They want to know what drugs you take. They want to know how you really think the Artist-Formerly-Known-as-Prince's symbol should be pronounced. That's how invasive it can get. So, of course, they want to know if you've ever seen a therapist. My initial reaction was, "*Oh my God*, if anybody is honest enough to admit they have a therapist, they would be admitting to being certifiable, and that would mean they were a risk to national security because they were going to blab all the government's secrets to the enemy and then they wouldn't get the clearance, which means they wouldn't get the job."

But then I found out that if you've received counselling, it actually gives you some credibility, actual security brownie points, because it means that you have sought to improve yourself and you've developed some self-awareness. I signed up *tout de suite* for some therapy not least because I thought it might counter that space bon-bon I ate in Amsterdam in 1998, but, yes, because I also thought it might actually help me. And guess what? It did!

In therapy, I got to feel what it's like to be entirely myself in a completely nonjudgemental space. It was probably the first time I felt completely safe telling my story exactly as it is without having to deal with someone else's reaction of horror, pity, disgust, or any other response that made me want to withdraw back to the safety of the masks. It was the first time I was able to observe parts of my true self and explore what lay underneath. It was the first time I had given myself permission to observe my truth, and it was liberating.

When you get out of touch with who you really are and what comes most naturally for you, you become someone who you don't feel you are and you start living someone else's story, not your own. You're essentially plagiarising. It's not a lie as such, but it's not the whole truth either. The version of yourself that you show people is a part of you, but it isn't the core of you, the real you, the *balanced* you. It isn't the you aligned with your purpose and your values and what you were put on this Earth to create. You might choose to tell your story differently for different audiences to get a different reaction, but they're all versions of the same thing. Even if you could, no one would be willing to stick around long enough to listen to the extended remix of who you are. So storytelling in life becomes a bit of a skill. You have to pick and choose which bits you're going to divulge for best effect and also to protect yourself.

Speaking of storytelling, do you ever complain about something by telling a story that focusses on the bad bits? Complaining is a very acceptable storytelling angle, frequently defended with some variation of "Because it's the truth!" But the good bits are equally true. When it comes to being authentic, it's important that you start with being honest with yourself about who you really are. And that's not just the shameful and sensationalistic bits. It includes the quality bits too. Your truth is a realistic appreciation of every part of yourself. As an exercise, try telling an alternative story about an event that happened to you and highlight the elements that you would prefer to focus on, such as the hope, the opportunities for growth, or— my favourite—the comedy. Pick a story in your own life that you've complained about recently and see how you can twist it to something more positive. How does it make you feel? Was it hard? If so, what part of you was making it difficult and is that telling you something about yourself?

Try it. It's fun. It will highlight how you currently perceive your reality and can also train you to frame your reality more to your liking. After all, they're all versions of the same truth. Maybe it'll also make you a more versatile storyteller too.

Now, truth-telling mustn't be confused with politeness. Politeness is where you're allowed to tell lies in the name of kindness. Politeness adds a whole new level of complexity to truth-telling. Politeness is a linguistically diverse sovereign state where *no* doesn't just mean *no* even when it sometimes means *yes*. It can also mean, "Pardon, what?" and "What else have you got on tap?" Politeness is *not* saying it like it is. As a coping mechanism, I like sharing stories of my run-ins with politeness with the sole intention of extracting similar stories from others. I might even set up an online thread dedicated to people sharing their best moments of politeness that had the most counterproductive effects, just so I can have 24/7 entertainment.

I'll start.

In my twenties, I was in a youth hostel in Canada having just travelled from the East Coast to the West Coast by car, and I had run out of money. I was literally down to my last twenty dollars before I was going to have to sleep out in the snow. I couldn't afford to eat more than a small tub of yoghurt a day, and I was very, very hungry.

I met another traveller from my dorm. She had bought a packet of macaroni and cheese for dinner. She said to me, as she shook the box, "There's too much in here for one person. Do you want to join me and we can share it together?"

At this point, a normal person might issue a silent prayer along the lines of "Thank you, oh legendary universe. You have not only given me a free feed in the nick of time, but it looks like I am also making a new friend. You rock."

But combine a lifetime of being told I should give and not take with the trait that a real lady never admits she is hungry (as fuck) because *that's not polite*, and I opened my mouth and out came, "No, thanks."

No.

No? Did I just reject a free meal? My body prodded me desperately, begging me to answer again and see if I couldn't get a better one on the second try. As if sensing my dilemma (or maybe she was looking at my concave stomach—she was a medical student, after all), the girl said, "Are you sure?" She shook the box again, enticingly.

I tried again, real hard this time. "I'm fine, thank you," I said. I even threw in a smile.

Gahhhh!

Conclusion: Politeness is a survival hazard. Surely if a person nearly starves to death in the name of politeness, that's when society has taken a construct too far.

Note how I've just blamed society for my inadequacies? More on that later. But wrapping up years of amateur politeness and trying not to offend people with my haphazard word choices and my oversharing—and untangling it all—is going to take some time. So when people tell me to "just be myself," as if it's as easy as opening a ring-pull can of tuna, I get a little triggered and respond with snarky remarks like, "Don't hold your breath, Buckface" and other well-chosen words like that.

As you become familiar with how you interpret your reality and start to shrug off the masks, keep coming back to the question, "Who am I right now? What is my truth in this moment?" Who you are is a state of being that shifts from one moment to the next. This is the universe's assurance that you will never run out of new things to discover about yourself, so the path to authenticity is, and pardon the cliché, a journey not a destination—it's a state of being, not an act of doing. It is easy to get bogged down in the details of how everyone else is not living in their truth, but that's just another attempt to avoid vulnerability. Your truth lies in observing all the ways your life has not turned out how you expected, admitting this to yourself, and observing the masks you have been wearing because of this disappointment and pain. With each new discovery, you are being true to yourself, and this gives you more courage to hold yourself steady.

Observing your masks allows you to identify all the ways you are compromising your truth to meet external demands. Dodging the truth in favour of politeness only compounds the suffering—and will never get you past your fears. Truth is foundational for authentic living and determining which parts of your identity are socially constructed and which parts are inherently you.

The meaning you assign to the events in your life is a combination of your beliefs and your feelings. Meaning bothers you when it feels bad and—in most human fashion—that's when you're least likely to accept that you might have the meaning wrong. I'll leave that there for you to interpret what it means for you while I quietly whisper an all-purpose mantra in your ear that can be used anytime you encounter life's foul situations: "What do you want it to mean?"

CHAPTER 5

DECIDE

You've now completed your current-state analysis. It's not so much done as you're done with it. In reality, there's no end to how much you can investigate your current state, especially given that it's not static. But you get to a point where you're out of time, money, patience, and/or curiosity, and you're ready to look at what's next. The analysis into how you feel, what you believe, and how you interpret your life will never end, so consider the skills and knowledge you acquired over the previous chapters as lifetime gifts that you will return to over and over as you evolve. Remember, this is not a linear process.

At the completion of a current-state analysis on an IT project, I usually hear a lot of fearful, chaotic juju around making decisions about the future. Despite newly acquired self-awareness and knowing the need for change, the "how?" and the "what first?" can get a bit overwhelming. Management are simultaneously rearing to go and terrified to make a move in case it's the wrong one. So this is where I usually throw around a little juju of my own that gets people moving toward the future state they desire without them knowing they're doing it. Part of this involves highlighting the habits and automatic behaviours that are keeping them stuck. So this chapter will get you thinking about some of your own habits and reactions so you can ponder how they influence your day-to-day decisions and your ability to move forward. Only it may not feel as magic as when I do it in IT because I've just blown my cover and revealed my methods.

ACTION AND PRIORITIES

Every time I take a serious look at what is most important in my life, I see just how many of my actions are out of alignment with my desires. I realise, for example, that I have spent an inordinate amount of energy avoiding being told that I'm doing a bad job. I have literally relocated myself geographically to avoid the possibility of people not liking what I'm doing and then having to experience that burning shame of not being good enough. When it comes to avoidance, I am a master. Had you asked me, though, what my priorities were in life, avoiding shame would not have been one of them. My actions were completely out of alignment with all that was important to me. Subconsciously, my number one priority was avoiding all the bad shit even though I believed I was being true to myself. Facing these realisations was not easy, and I had to challenge myself to stop making excuses for why I acted the way I did. I had to see my motivation for what it was and not what I wanted it to be. I had to ask myself why I was avoiding the discomfort of failure, why I kept trying to hide. I had to become comfortable in the uncomfortable, and it was not easy. But when I can see how my actions are out of alignment with my values and my truth, I experience less internal conflict and less overall dissatisfaction with my life. My decisions become more meaningful, and I encounter compounding growth. By practising radical honesty and living in alignment, you will gain a deeper understanding of your desires and your motivations, which will equip you to live your truth out loud.

Have an unbiased look at your actions and whether they are aligned with what is most important to you. Are any hidden motivations propelling you forward: "Where am I saying one thing but doing another? Do my recent actions reflect my truth? If not, what is the motivation for why I act the way I do? What am I afraid of?" There will be some pesky old beliefs rattling your cage in there, for sure.

Your deepening ability to self-reflect is your new best friend. So keep moving. Every chance you get, do one thing each day that feels aligned with your convictions, no matter how small, even if the rest of what you're doing still has kinks and twists. Do something you want to do, that you love to do, and make it something that's possible right now. (By the way, just thinking about what you want to do doesn't count.)

If you can't think of anything, stop for a second. There are times where no matter how hard you look, there really is nothing you want, like when you're hungry and the only thing on offer is a platter of pickled shark. In these cases, be still. Take the next sixty seconds to regroup and acknowledge what's going on. Sit with your feelings of stuckness, of overwhelm and indecision. Let them flow through your body. Allowing yourself to experience your emotions is alignment; it is also authenticity. Give them time to pass. Observe them without judgement. That alone will release you. Sometimes that's what you need most in moments you feel stuck or confused. Even ten seconds helps if that's all you've got. I was serious when I said pick something no matter how small. When you allow yourself to do this, it's like activating a reset switch; often, you can then look back at your current circumstances and see options you didn't notice before. Holding yourself accountable to making one small decision, taking one small action, sets you in motion. It is often fear that prevents people from starting, fear that makes people procrastinate. But changing your life, becoming your authentic self, means taking brave steps into fear and not away from it. It may feel as though you don't know what you want, but fear is often the culprit behind indecision. Take a moment to feel your fear without acting on it and allow yourself to connect with your truth. Disarming your fear in this way allows you to see more clearly. You might even discover a chicken nugget nestled in amongst the pickled fish.

You can change yourself and your reality by moving out of your head and taking a break from yourself even if for a few moments.

FOCUS

There's a saying that goes, "Where focus goes, energy flows." Attention is like an electrical current. Whatever you focus on—whether you're thinking about it, looking at it, or engaging with it in any other way—receives power from you. The emotion you're feeling is like the voltage and this transfers to your target, setting up a relationship between you and it. The more you focus on this thing with that same emotion, the stronger the association between the target and your feelings will become.

Imagine you're starting a new job, and every time you think about the job, you feel excited. This will strengthen the association of excitement with the job. The more you think about the job alongside this feeling, the more that positive vibration will fuel everything about the job in your reality. If you're feeling fearful about your new job, however, and this is the dominant emotion you feel every time you think about work, then this feeling will extend to the way you experience your work, until you decide to change it. And you can change it.

Turn your awareness to how you're feeling when you focus on the things in your life. Observing this relationship can give you clarity as to why some things aren't turning out for you the way you would like them to, and why others come so easily. What's your relationship like with money, for example? Or the way you look? Or the way your body functions?

Just like electricity, your attention needs a target. Try focussing on nothing. Pretty hard, right? I heard a YouTuber once talking about the fact that people tend to fixate on things, particularly the bad stuff. She likened life to a buffet. You take your plate, walk along the selection of food, pick out the stuff you want to eat, and put it on your plate. Suddenly, you come across something you don't want and think, "Eww, I would never eat that." You then stand there staring at it, thinking, "I don't want that! That's gross!" You want to tell people how much you don't want it, how offensive it is that it's even sitting there for you to see, how you can't imagine that anybody could eat it, and that anyone who does put it on their plate is a dickhead. You stand around waiting for someone to put it on their plate so you can tell them they're a dickhead. Meanwhile, everyone's moving past you, having a really good time putting what they want onto their plates and going back to their tables to enjoy their meals while you're stuck staring at what you don't want.

When you're riding a bike and you see a pothole, you have to look away; otherwise you will end up in the hole. So if you find yourself focussing on things that you associate with negative feelings, then you have two options. Three, actually, because one option is always to stay exactly as you are. Who am I to judge whether you want to end up in a pothole or not? But for the times where you don't, here are your two options:

The first and easiest is to shift your focus onto something else that makes you feel better. This is particularly useful for unwanted thoughts. For example, imagine five times a day you still find yourself worrying about that steak you embarrassingly overcooked for friends last year and, now, anytime you think about steak, you feel shame. In these cases, you can pre-prepare an alternative thought that triggers a more positive feeling, so you can shift deftly without having to frantically scan your environment for a better one on the fly. Next time the thought of steak pops into your head, you can now instantly switch to an image of your famous Chicken Rendang that everybody loves. The idea is to have a plan for when the intrusive thought arrives. This is also a form of reframing. Rather than focussing on your perceived failure, you turn your mind to a success you have experienced. This allows you to reframe the beliefs you associate with that thought or feeling; for example, changing "I am a terrible cook" to "People love my food, I am a great cook, it was just the one time I overcooked the steak!" The difference is where you choose to focus.

Another option, and you can use this in conjunction with the diversion option above, is to use it as an opportunity for growth. As in the previous chapters, if you have a negative association with something, then there is an opportunity there to investigate the underlying belief that is fuelling it, and take this as the first step toward changing it.

Use the rule of thumb that any belief that makes you fearful or scared—or any of the negative emotions that you don't wish to feel—is a false belief. Yep, it's a bold statement. But it's true. The soul's natural state is bliss, joy, and love. When you are feeling bad, this obscures the love, impeding the natural flow, like the clouds blocking the sun, which is always shining even behind a gloomy day. You can choose to raise your energy frequency above the clouds and back to the blissful joy, which is always there, if you are willing to shift your focus. Start to view these negative feelings as a signpost for the change that your human is craving and your soul is guiding you to.

Occasionally, no matter which way you turn, it might feel like you just can't escape something. When my brother and I were little, we used to play a game where he would have to block my path in the hallway and I would try to escape. He was stronger and faster than me, and I never won. Given this, I realised there was one major flaw in the rules: The game couldn't end until my brother decided it would. I could push and shove and yell and scream as much as I liked, but I was stuck until he decided to let me go. Comparing his staying power as a little boy to the gentle soul he has become, I still can't figure out how he turned out okay—my only explanation is that sometimes you have to see who you're not to find out who you are. Anyway, tangent. My point is that sometimes there is no escape. And, exactly like the earlier example in Actions and Priorities, when you can't find anything you want, that's when you close your eyes and turn your focus inward. Stop pushing and shoving for a moment, find the inner peace, and lay your focus there. That was the one tactic I never tried as a kid. If only I'd known.

STANDARDS AND BOUNDARIES

Live by your standards, enforce your boundaries. Get frank and fearless, upfront and personal, down in the weeds, and all the other sayings about setting your own boundaries and living by your chosen standards. Never has showing up as your authentic self required so much courage as it does when you have to consistently live by your own standards and enforce your boundaries. Standards, and the non-negotiable boundaries that define them, are the parameters to your life that define your truth and the way in which you live your truth. This approach empowers you to make authentic decisions that align with your true self and what feels comfortable for you rather than succumbing to external pressures or expectations and allowing these to define your reality. One of my standards is that I don't start work before 11:00 a.m. My actions and decisions reflect this standard, and I am not swayed by temptations of workshops, meetings, or deadlines that happen before this time no matter how exciting they may seem. As a result, people now know that this is how I operate in the same way they know other things about me, such as how I snack all day long and I never wear long dresses. My standards have become just like my other personal traits that everybody recognises as a part of me. As a result, I rarely need to enforce my boundaries.

Maintaining your own standards on a daily basis, and enforcing your boundaries where necessary, sends a message to the world about who you are, what you're willing to tolerate, and what you're not. When somebody oversteps one of your boundaries, standing your ground can feel very uncomfortable, so living by your own standards is, in many ways, a much easier way to avoid being pushed beyond your limits. Choosing to live by your own standards without exception allows others to get to know the real you, and it is your first line of defence against being pulled out of your authenticity. When people see you living by your standards, and they come to know you like this, they are far less likely to encroach on your boundaries. Instead, they'll understand your non-negotiables, and they'll treat you accordingly.

So let's then have a look at what happens when standards are not consistently upheld and somebody bites through your crispy outer shell into the gooey centre.

It's an ode to the nice girl. She's the one who I was trying to be the whole time I was growing up and well into my adulthood. She's the one the older generations adored. The nice girl speaks quietly. She never swears, and if she does, she feels very ashamed of herself and apologises profusely. Nice girls don't enjoy swearing as much as I used to. Nice girls should also agree to everything as if it's so easy and it's what they actually want because being disagreeable isn't nice. That includes letting a boy pat your bum or kiss you even if you don't want him to because otherwise he might get offended. People feel good around someone who loves their ideas, who laughs at all their jokes, who does what they want to do, so the nice girl does all these things because that's what will make her popular; it's what will get her the job and make her friends, and that's what will keep the peace and avoid people feeling confronted. The nice girl also doesn't laugh too loudly, and if she does crack a joke, it's a polite one that doesn't outshine anybody else's jokes, particularly those of the men because they're better at humour than women. The nice girl isn't sexy when she's being funny because nobody wants to shag the comedian. And a whole bunch of other limiting beliefs that have created a very interesting culture to inhabit.

If you are or have been the nice girl, do you have anything to say to her? I know I do. I want to tell her that the only men she'll be happy with think she is sexy for her humour, and that the job she wants to get paid her worth for, and to be really happy in, values her point of view and doesn't fire her when she provides constructive feedback on the way they operate because they need people who can contribute in that way. The people who want to hire her do so *because* she can speak out and maybe even because she likes to swear; maybe that's who they are too, and they feel comfortable around somebody who speaks their truth because it gives them licence to do so as well. The job she doesn't want is the job she takes only because she's scared that she won't find anything better or isn't good enough for more. That's not the vibe she wants when going for the interview. And it's the same type of thing for the dating circuit. These are all standards your authentic self lives by, and you have to be the one who maintains them.

I'm grateful to the nice girl, though, because by showing me who she is, I've seen who I'd rather be. She's taken me so far away from my authentic self at times that, in frustration and anger, I pushed back and discovered my real power. Because she has allowed my boundaries to be violated time and time again, I can see very clearly what my standards need to be. So I have learned many lessons from her, but the one thing she can't give me is the strength to apply those lessons. That has to come from the real me because all nice girls can do about that is to giggle and say, "Boundary? Don't be silly, I can't see any boundaries."

If you're like me, and you've spent a significant part of your life not living by your own standards, then it's quite possible that you have interpreted anybody who violates your boundaries as rude and offensive, insensitive, and as someone who doesn't know where to draw the line. If you are not enforcing and delineating your boundaries, yet somehow still expecting others to know and respect them, then you may have negative associations with your boundaries from the pain and disrespect of having them trampled in the past. Suddenly choosing to impose these boundaries can trigger these same feelings and can, therefore, be just as uncomfortable as if you're allowing somebody to violate them. But only to start with. The more you respect your own standards, the more you heal, the healthier you will get, and the benefits quickly start to outweigh any of those echoes from the past.

SELF-ACCEPTANCE

Just like the current-state analysis, who you are right now is fact. Many times, when looking at the current-state analysis that's been done on a project, management read it aghast and implore me to change it to something more appetising. It's hard accepting every part of yourself, but accepting the truth is not only a necessary first step to moving forward, it's *the* process of moving forward. Wrap your brain around that one. It's also useful to know that who you are now doesn't have to affect who you can be tomorrow or even who you will be in an hour's time. This is the nature of authenticity—it's a moment-by-moment thing.

So it's easy to think at this point that you are not ready to start your transformation because you're not quite the squeaky-clean person you want to be when starting such an important chapter in your life. Perhaps you want to leave behind that annoying argumentative trait you have because that's not spiritual or enlightened and it will interfere with your decisions. And so will your gruffness toward little kids, and the fact that you sleep in and waste half of the day. You're already worrying about how you will get up and meditate for a couple of hours like a yogi and be kind to animals if you only roll out of bed at 11:00 a.m. and have to rush straight to work.

But you've come this far and you've already seen, heard, and pondered so much. You can't un-know any of that stuff, and, as a result, your journey has already started. Your spirit is already awakening, and there is no putting it back to sleep. Whether or not you are aware of it, you already know so much more about who you really are and how you really think and feel than when you started, and that's all the journey is. The journey to authenticity is the journey to self-acceptance and vice versa. Besides, to accept yourself for who you are, you need to have something to accept, and, obviously, it's got to be something that you don't already accept. Otherwise, there's no journey, you're not going anywhere. It's easy enough to accept your perfectly shaped legs and your PhD-educated mind, but it's not as easy to accept the dark side of you that hides food from your family and lies to her husband about how much money she's earning so she can spend more on makeup.

I classify my "bad" traits into two categories. The first are the socially acceptable ones, such as refusing to peel my own oranges or talking when I've been specifically told to shut up. These are the types I'll admit to. Then there's the second category, the ones that induce terror, for fear that they might come out into the open and ruin me. Everyone has these types and knows which ones they are. Enough said.

The journey to authenticity requires your whole self—integrating the good and the bad, and the dark and the light. It is putting back together the fractured parts of yourself, the rejected and shamed parts of yourself, the parts you don't want anyone to see. The courage I've mentioned throughout these pages is obtained by learning how to hold the light and the dark sides of yourself simultaneously. There is tremendous strength in being able to say, "Experiencing this part of myself feels like shit, but I'm still okay." You must bring your shadows with you. Shadows are essential to the learning journey, and, as your soul will attest, those shadows have been strategically placed there for you to give you a puzzle to solve, to give you something to do in this lifetime so that you actually get out of bed each day and evolve.

So now you're heading into the fun part, the juicy part, and there's nothing you have to do before you go. There's nothing to think about first, nothing you need to psych yourself up for. In fact, the less mentally prepared you are, the better. Feeling mentally prepared is akin to having your armour on, and that's a guaranteed way to hinder the process. Have you ever been on one of those rides at an amusement park where you are taken to a great height and then dropped into a free fall? The one I went on lifted me up fifteen storeys and, at the top, there was a digital countdown on a screen. It started at five, then four, and my adrenaline was pumping, three, I was freaking out, two, burping up my lunch. Then we dropped. They dropped us two seconds early just to make sure we . . . I don't know, but that's what they did.

Being unprepared has its advantages. It strips away your protective layer and exposes your true self. It sounds scary, I know, but you're reading a book, not being dropped from a height. How bad can it be? Make the choice to accept yourself as you are in this moment, radical acceptance without conditions or judgement, as you move into this next chapter. You are becoming the highest version of yourself. You don't have to wait until you are a "better person" to start giving yourself what you deserve. Allowing yourself to have what you love makes you a better person, not the other way around. All you have to do is decide.

You're now armed with even more insight into where you behave unconsciously and how this influences your life. When you choose to live more consciously, then each conscious action becomes a decision point where you can choose what you do instead of being dragged there involuntarily by your old habits. If this sounds overwhelming, then yeah, I agree, there's a lot of information in there, so take your time, slow everything right down, and feel your way into it. And keep reminding yourself that life is lived in each moment, not in the goals you set for yourself. No matter how fast or slow you try to go, life is still only happening at the same speed.

CHAPTER 6

DREAM

I n IT, creating the future state is a serious activity where everything is defined in minute detail, no stone left unturned, and nobody makes a move until everybody agrees on what is being done. It's a very rigorous, structured process.

Who am I kidding? It's the most chaotic clusterfuck if ever there was, but if you read the manual, it'll tell you the step-by-step process toward obtaining an exquisite set of future-state requirements that will make everything perfect and people happy—where nature and harmony rule over the kingdom once again. But luckily, you're not an IT system. You're a creative, dynamic being for whom unstructured dreaming is innate. Dreaming, along with imagination and a good hit of feminine energy, are the traits you need to expand into the highest version of yourself. This is the part where you go somewhere new and you become that next-level you. So don't skimp on how or what you dream about. And definitely don't make it a rigid process. Let it rip. It's one of the few places you can.

DISCO DANCING AND HOVERBOARDS

When I was about five years old, my grandmother took me to her next door neighbour's house for a barbecue. There were some other girls there who were a little older than me, and when a song came on the radio, they jumped up and started doing a choreographed dance. It was the first time I'd ever seen anything like it, and I was mesmerised. I thought it was the most amazing thing I'd ever seen, and all I knew was that that's what I wanted to do. I couldn't stop staring. It was as if I were looking into my future, and, in that moment, that was my whole life. I said to my grandmother, "Those girls, I want that. I want to do that. I need to be like them."

I was desperate, and was obviously talking about it so much that when my grandmother dropped me home that night, she told my mother, "Kate saw some girls doing ballet today, and she really liked it."

Ballet. She had probably never seen anyone pulling disco moves either. So seeing the crazed passion in my eyes and how inspired I was, my mother immediately took action and enrolled me in a classical ballet class.

So I turned up to my first lesson, and I had the ballet shoes and the leotard and the tights, and I learnt to do first position, second position, and how to point my toes. And at the end of the lesson, my mother asked how it went. And I said, "Well, I haven't learned to do what those girls at the barbecue were doing yet. So that was a bit disappointing."

And my mother said, "You have to be patient because it takes time to learn those sorts of moves. You've got to learn the basics first. If you keep going and you do what the teacher tells you, I'm sure you will learn whatever it is you saw those girls doing; I'm sure that's what you'll end up doing."

So I took my mother's word for it, and I mustered all the patience a six-year-old can muster. And for three whole years, I learnt classical ballet, and there was not a single disco move. Not a single disco song played the whole time.

Are your dreams still your own creation, and how much might they have been distorted by somebody else's reality?

There is a lesson that I took away from the ballet experience that I didn't apply straight away. In the eighties, when I started watching futuristic movies that promised me an adulthood full of hoverboards and flying cars, or when I bought into the docudrama that getting a good job meant a suit, an office, a computer, and getting up early, I took it all very literally. So once I got the job that looked good on LinkedIn, I was like, "How patient do I have to be before I get my hoverboard, cause I don't feel like I'm flying yet?"

I usually said this pretty quietly so that the nice girl didn't hear me because she used to say, "Don't let them hear you being so ungrateful." And then she would proceed to pull starving children in Africa into the conversation to make me feel extra bad.

Simultaneously, though, that disco-dancing child was always inside me bellowing, "WHEN??"

Turns out, I've already got a hoverboard. Not a literal hoverboard— it's better than that. I've got the feeling inside me that I always felt when I imagined myself riding one. I know how I want to feel, and I've felt that feeling heaps of times. I've had the tools to make my own hoverboard-like experience all these years, but instead I've been sitting around waiting for someone else to do it for me. I've been patiently waiting for someone to teach me disco moves and tolerating classical ballet in the meantime. But no more. I'm going hoverboarding. No one's ever seen the hoverboard I've got in my mind, so when I first do my hoverboarding impression, some people are going to look at me and say, "What the fuck are you doing? That's not a hoverboard." Meanwhile, though, I will be having an awesome time doing the thing that makes me feel like I used to when I watched those eighties movies. Other people, people who get it, look at me and see me having an awesome time and say, "Go you! That's how it's done!" The people who think your hoverboard is stupid just aren't your people. You want to focus on the people who see you as someone who is doing something you love, not as someone who is being weird. If you know what I'm talking about, then you are my people.

So, no, I never ended up being a professional *Solid Gold* dancer, but by reframing my perspective, disco dancing was still in my future just as that little girl imagined; it just manifested as an important lesson that had the most profound impact on my life. That's a passable twist, don't you think?

ABOUT TIME

Thank God quantum physics has made some inroads into time travel since I was a kid because, along with hoverboards and flying cars, I just assumed that time travel would be a given in my future. Since those days, however, my imagination has really taken a hit from my narrow view of reality, and it's taken some effort to get it back up to speed so that I could see the personal benefits to be had from what the latest in science was telling me. With the realisation that reality is so much more than what I perceive it to be, I had to turbo-charge my imagination so I could expand from the reality I currently hold into the reality that I wanted, in all its juicy potential.

For thousands of years, Eastern and spiritual philosophy has been saying that there is no past and no future, that everything is happening at once, and that The Now is all that exists. Even bog-standard science is saying that time is not linear, that it can bend, speed up, and slow down—that time's trajectory is influenced by the person perceiving it, which essentially means that time as you know it only exists in your head and not in any absolute form out there in the universe. Given that everybody is living in different realities of their own construction, and there is no such thing as absolute truth or reality, then it makes sense that time falls into that bucket as well.

So if you can get on board with the fact that time doesn't exist, then suddenly the concept of time travel doesn't look nearly as far-fetched as it used to. This is a very useful attitude to have—not because you're hanging out for the day where you can buckle into your DeLorean and go back to unsay that bad thing you once said to your maths teacher—but because it helps stretch your imagination about what's possible. You want to get your imagination to the point where you can say "anything is possible" and really mean it. You will need the strongest, buffest imagination if you're going to take advantage of what The Now has to offer. Remember, there was a time when the Earth really was flat. It really was. Because if nothing exists other than what's in your mind, and nobody thought that the Earth was round, then the Earth couldn't have been round because nobody thought it. I love how much that fucks with my mind.

Maybe the universe snuck a little bowl of "time-does-not-exist" onto the buffet to remind you to keep some magic in your life, some mystery, to keep things interesting, to keep you dreaming, and to make humans invent the stuff that they're yet to invent. Maybe there was once "the-Earth-is-round" in that same bowl many years ago that most people couldn't fathom putting on their plate for fear of puking. Either way, I'm eyeing up that little bowl, and I'm looking around for the waiter so I can ask for a bigger plate.

Now that you've ascertained that nothing exists, including time, because there is no reality other than the one you construct in your own mind, take a leaf out of the mindfulness handbook and come entirely into the present, or the quantum field of potentiality (which is the term I prefer because it's got more fizz to it; simply put, this term refers to the idea that, in the present moment, all possibilities and outcomes exist), and observe its infinite potential. In this moment, you are poised to move in any direction you want, make any decision you want, and make any dream come true. In the very next moment, you can be anyone at all. You are limited only by what you believe and what you desire.

The idea that anything is possible, literally, can help you to see beyond your immediate reality and its constraints and limitations. Dreaming is a part of discovering your soul's purpose. Without it, you remain where you are. It is rooted in this philosophy: That there are an infinite number of possible designs for your life and that your existence is dynamic and evolving. Anything can be yours, if you are bold enough to dream.

CONSTRUCT YOUR OWN GOD

In some ways I'd rather be talking to a group of teenage boys about menstrual cups and haemorrhoids than about this next topic because at least it would be less controversial. But I feel this has to be said. I feel there needs to be a conversation about the artist and well-known personality commonly referred to as God, also known as Creator, Allah, Source, Universe, Spirit, All That Is, Mother Nature, and numerous other terms that ultimately refer to some form of higher consciousness and which carry such heightened meaning for so many people that it's hard to say or even write the word on any objective or common level, but here goes anyway.

In his famous TED Talk, Ken Robinson tells a story of a little girl drawing a picture at school and her teacher asking her, "What is that a picture of?"

The little girl replies, "It's a picture of God," to which the teacher says, "But nobody knows what God looks like."

The little girl turns back to her drawing and says, "They will in a minute."

One reason I used to get so agitated by organised religion is that it involved somebody else telling me what I should believe, and I always found that really irritating. For that reason, I stubbornly refused for many years to entertain the possibility of any sort of higher power. I mean, occasionally, I would stumble across a spiritual idea that I really liked, but I was told I couldn't just buy the one, I had to get the entire set. It was all or nothing. These discoveries usually ended with me leaving the idea at the sales counter without paying and storming out in a huff.

As you're rebuilding your whole philosophical framework, flushing all the beliefs that you don't want in your world down the mental toilet—the ones that don't work for you, the ones you don't like, the ones you never liked and that never liked you—then before you pour the slab, add in anything that'll ensure your new beliefs are robust enough to allow you to experience your reality the way you want to. Everything that I'm talking about in this book has been said thousands of times before, and for thousands of years, and you will find that these concepts are applied in science, psychology, medicine, the Koran, the Bible, New Age spiritual affirmations, the law, energy healing—you name it, it's all the same thing at the core, just presented from a different marketing angle with different headings and with different branding.

Once I realised that my spiritual framework could be like a Choose Your Own Adventure story where I could have whatever I wanted and leave out the stuff I didn't like, I got really excited. I was like, "So I can have *that*? And that? And that as well? Can I have that without that? And not that, ever?" Because that's who I am, that's my identity. I got to construct a reality that resonated with me. I would hear things and say, "My God, yes! That's so aligned with me, I want that!" My reality became something that I was in love with, and suddenly the impossible started to look possible. My belief framework became something that was going to support me in achieving my dreams instead of something to hold me back for fear of getting it wrong and not fitting in.

If all possibilities exist, then God is whoever you think God is. This means that constructing a spiritual framework that allows you to achieve your dreams and your potential is not just okay, it's necessary. You are free to dream. Question the value of holding on to spiritual beliefs that keep you playing small, that force you to accept a reality where you are fundamentally a bad person and unworthy of good things. Flush them down the belief toilet and choose a spiritual reality that feels authentic to you, choose a God who is aligned with your highest self, and trust that you have an ancient and deep knowing within you that really knows the truth. Spiritual awakening is about returning back to this truth, not shaping a truth around external expectations and projections. Dreams are how you access the mystery, how you open yourself up to the limitless potential that is available within you, placed there by a higher power that created you to have it all. Your life, in all its uniqueness, is an expression of God.

ABUNDANCE VERSUS LACK

Your ability to dream big is influenced by your belief of what is possible, which, ironically, kind of defeats the purpose of dreaming. One of the biggest blocks to dreaming is the mindset of lack, the belief that there isn't enough. The universe knows that there's enough, that everything is in abundance; it's your human belief that there is not enough that creates situations of lack in your physical reality.

One of society's all-time best-selling lack beliefs is There's Not Enough Time. Most of the adults in my community subscribe to this one. When I was a kid, we had a family subscription, and we used to analyse it around the dinner table the way Christians study the Bible. We would interpret it in the context of our day and look for different ways to assimilate its lessons into our lives. That belief alone has made society a lot of money. Not surprisingly, it's probably been instrumental in some cultures becoming some of the wealthiest in the world. People who buy Not Enough Time often also purchase Not Enough Money, Not Enough Food for Everybody in The World, and Not Enough Being Done About Climate Change.

From an early age, I heard all of these lack beliefs reflected in conversations within my own household, at school, on TV, and in the enormous number of books I read because Xbox didn't exist yet. This exposure generated some of my own creations of lack: Not Enough Sleep, Not Enough Playdates, and, my favourite, Not Enough Topping on My Ice Cream.

Learning that there was not enough for me and for others made me feel like I was a burden on my family and society. It taught me to play small, not ask for what I needed, and limit my dreams to something mainstream and familiar that wouldn't encroach on anybody else's dreams. Talk about not showing up as my authentic self.

I learned to define myself in smaller terms than what I really was so that I didn't take up too much space because if I did show up as the more expansive me, there might not be enough left for somebody else. Enough of what, it wasn't clear, but this is where the lack belief begins.

Most people have programmed their brains to default to "there's not enough" even when there is, justifying it by explaining that this is how you take care of the things you value most—by not wasting them. So you have to apportion them out and use them wisely. If you use them too liberally, you're being greedy, thoughtless, and not leaving enough for everyone else. So you are sparing with your love, your attention, your happiness, and your fun in the belief that they are finite. And as a result, you experience a lack of time, of headspace, of variety, of patience, of willpower, of energy, of interest, of solutions, and of success. Lack begets lack, and just like the politeness epidemic, I feel the lack mindset has been taken way too far. It's colouring language and attitudes, and this manifests actual situations of lack in the physical world, like inequality, which leads to even more devastating situations of lack, such as poverty, war, and famine.

A few years ago, I was invited to speak at a girls' high school in Sydney. At the end of my talk, one of the students asked for information on a government department for which I had done some work. Other students were also interested, and I wasn't surprised. This was a very sought-after department, and they have an extremely sexy graduate program. There were many things to share about this department, all of them true, but my initial thought was to lament that the program was very competitive and only a handful of the thousands of applicants each year are successful. This speaks volumes to the default lack mentality constantly idling in the background, which seems to skip the queue ahead of other, more empowering, but equally valid facts. Just as true, but much more likely to motivate school leavers to follow their dreams, were the words that, luckily,

I chose to say instead: "It is a first-class program, graduates are guaranteed a fast-tracked career, they get to travel the world, and they are provided with exclusive training and an opportunity to work in every area of the department during the year-long program to decide which areas they love the most." I reckon those words are so much more inspiring than me sucking on my teeth and saying, "Well, just prepare yourself for disappointment."

Based on this philosophy, an abundance mindset fosters the belief that, like the quantum field of potentiality, there are limitless possibilities for your life and for your dreams. Rather than operating from the framework of lack, abundance tells you that there is more than enough in the world, and you are allowed to have it. Dreams, opportunities, change, happiness. Whatever aligns with your dreams is yours for the taking. When you believe that resources are plentiful, you will become more resourceful, finding ways to leverage what you have to accomplish your goals. This is the power of an abundance mindset when you are dreaming with an intent to create a new reality for yourself. Living from a space of lack will not propel you forward, no matter how valiant you think your cause. Being a martyr only hurts your own personal growth and development and won't win you any favours. If you are serious about changing your life, start with the belief that maybe, just maybe, you have been holding yourself back all along in an effort to be the nice girl. And maybe, just maybe, you aren't inherently bad and don't need redemption. Maybe your very life should be an expression of the abundance available to everyone.

THE COLOUR OF GRATITUDE

All the best human experiences on the planet have been watered down at some point by a platitude. It wasn't intentional. I mean, I get it: You have a really intense experience and you want to share it, to talk about it—but once it gets talked about and shared over and over again, it kind of loses its potency. Bumper stickers and crochet wall hangings can inspire in their own right, but the true sentiment behind it all is often long gone.

There's one sentiment, though, that I want to dust off and glam up for you. See if you can guess what it is. Take a look at all the things that you've got in your life, and focus on the bits that if you didn't have them, you'd be lost—the parts of your life you never have to worry about, except when you're having a moment, and then you worry about not having them and feel really bad and scared. They are things that if you didn't have them, you would spend endless amounts of time lamenting to your friends about how your life is so meaningless without these things.

Make a list of them all and see what emotion comes to mind when you think about how much meaning they have for you. Yep, you guessed right, I'm talking about gratitude. Okay smarty pants, so you knew already because I put it in the heading, but nonetheless, gratitude, like all the other platitudes, has become at best a social nicety rather than an intense emotion that has the power to draw you to all the things you desire in your life.

Remember when you were a kid and perhaps you were told to list of all the things you were grateful for, and then you had to reel them off, maybe kneeling by the bed while saying your prayers: Thank you God for my cat, thank you God for Mummy and Daddy, thank you God for my brother and my sister. Like you really meant it. It was typically a list of the things that you felt you should be grateful for, and you did it as quickly as possible so you could get off the cold floorboards and into bed. You didn't really get the value of the exercise, but you did it anyway because you were told to. That's not the gratitude I'm talking about—that's a list. The gratitude I'm referring to is a feeling, and a really big one. In fact, gratitude, along with love, has one of the most powerful vibrational frequencies in the universe.

This is how I visualise the power of emotional frequencies: Were you ever told as a kid that there was a special chemical in the swimming pool that would turn the water purple if you peed in it? I always imagined weeing in the pool and a big purple cloud appearing behind me, and I was terrified that even the smallest drop would seep out and I would be exposed. That's what emotions are like. If you could see emotions, they'd emanate from you like the wee in the pool, different colours for each emotion, and they would float out into the water and other people would swim through them, and particles of them would land in people's hair and on their skin. Your emotions are never just about you. It doesn't matter what you're saying or doing in an attempt to mask your true feelings; that colourful puddle of emotion is still floating about in the pool and influencing people and their behaviour. So, with this in mind, what emotions are people consuming from you, and is that how you want to colour your community?

Gratitude has a magnetic quality. It smells nicer, its colour is brighter, it travels further, and its particles have a more powerful effect when they land. When you feel gratitude, you vibrate at a higher frequency, and this energy has a positive effect on the vibration of others. If gratitude were a superhero, it would have the power to heal and to turn thoughts into reality. Feeling gratitude as often as you possibly can is the key to creating the masterpiece you desire for your life. It's like a magic portal that can take you wherever you want to go. No joke. Remember how the brain is a programmable instrument that literally programs itself by repetition? You especially want to hard-code gratitude. It's one for the swag bag.

Now, I know that you know you should be grateful for shit. I'm not telling you how to suck eggs, but what I am saying is that gratitude is a feeling, not a list, and it's time to become more aware of the presence of the feeling and feel that feeling at a much deeper level. And yeah, it will also help if you make a list.

Abundance and gratitude work hand in hand. Think of something you've already got in your life, something that fills your cup to the point that you can't even conceive what more of it would look like. Everyone's got something in their life that they feel they have more than enough of, an abundance of. Initially, you might have to go for a bit of a hunt, especially if you've been staring too long at the devilled egg on the buffet that you don't want. Consider the big and the small stuff in your life in equal measure. They all hold power in your life. Do you have a freckle on your wrist that you like the shape of? The smell of the air as the sun sets? Or the way your child places his hand on the back of yours when he wants to ask you a question?

As you start doing an inventory of your life, you will find things you don't think about anymore even though there was a time when you first got them and you were so excited that you went into overdrive. It was like, "Oh my God, I can NOT believe this is happening!" I think that about my husband. All those years ago, when I first realised that he was interested in me, I couldn't believe a guy like that would actually like me, and I very nearly blew a fuse when I found out he did. But now that we've been married for twenty years, I'm like, well sure, of course he likes me, yeah, so? But if we didn't still feel the same way about each other, I'd be really worried. When I think about not having him in my life, I go into a tailspin. I try not to think about that too much. The purpose of the exercise is, after all, to feel good. But reflecting on what your life will look like without the thing you have become so comfortable around can help you to conjure up more gratitude for it.

The well-known professor and social worker Brené Brown writes that gratitude is a perfect antidote for feelings of lack, especially the anxiety you feel when you worry about losing something you love. Gratitude is a wonderful tool to pull you out of that downward spiral. It's also really relaxing and calming, producing dopamine and serotonin, the body's feel-good chemicals, and reducing cortisol, the body's stress hormone. It's like a brain massage or a private smooch with yourself. If you're waiting at the bus stop, need to take a moment because you're feeling overwhelmed, or even when you're in that headspace where you don't know what to do with yourself, sit down, relax your body, and scroll through the things in your life, big and small, that really make you feel good, that you love to pieces, that make you feel love or peace or bliss or relaxation or delight, the things that make you cry with happiness, and really allow all those feel-good emotions to course through your body. And then amplify them with your thoughts. Put the emotion on a loop by continuing to focus on the things you love.

A grateful mindset also helps you bounce back from setbacks. Consider it part of your mental immune system that protects you from unwanted thoughts, a negative mindset, and lack of creativity. When you reflect on your progress over time and all the ways you have overcome past challenges by acknowledging what you have in your life that is good and worth celebrating, you will reframe your perspective to focus on your resilience and your ability to make good decisions, face hard things, and follow your dreams and thrive. Gratitude shifts the focus away from what you might not get right in the future toward what you have already done right in the past. This is how you improve your self-belief and give yourself a chance to dream bold dreams and build the life you are longing for.

So I guess the motivational posters and the Pope were right when they said express gratitude daily. If you need a boost or help getting started, I've got a no-sweat-blood-or-tears video on my website, kateangel.com, to get you into the vibe so that you never have to recite a list of items ever again and wonder why your life isn't working out.

Give yourself permission to dream in ways that are so wild and free that you could never share it with anybody. Stretch your imagination using your biggest, broadest mindset and all the magical things that grab your attention and light you up. The process of expanding your consciousness into new places is simultaneously showing you who you really are and creating your higher self.

CHAPTER 7

PLAY

READY GET SET GO

Have you ever signed up for a course simply because you want to learn to do something really cool? Like an anchor grind on a skateboard or perfecting the symmetrical steamed dim sum? You've seen other people doing it, you've fantasised about being able to do it, and you've imagined what it will feel like once you can do it, so now you just want to be doing it. But when you start the course, they tell you that first you have to learn the theory, the safety procedures, the history, and the socio-economic implications of skating technology in twentieth-century Europe, and all that stuff? Okay, now take a look in your swag bag. You've filled it with some pretty groovy stuff so far. You've got your abundance mentality, your reframing and storytelling skills, your spirit level to make sure your thoughts, feelings, beliefs, decisions, and actions are all in alignment, as well as your emotional navigational equipment. I've talked about some personal things, I've touched on toilets and pooping, uncomfortable feelings, mistakes and misunderstandings. I've cried with gratitude, given ultimatums, and told you a couple of times to get over yourself. I've sworn at you and talked for a second time about toilets. But all that stuff, that's all background info. It's the theory about uplevelling your life. You've done the hard yards, and now it's time to actually do the thing. You're going outside to have some fun.

The universe invented fun. It invented the sense of humour, the slapstick joke, comedy skits, and snorting when you laugh. The universe also invented bad moods, Internet trolls, and standing out in the rain because you're feeling too shitty to come inside and get warm by the fire. It also invented getting warm by the fire. It invented it all, and all of it is equally available to you to engage with in any way you choose. The universe does not care which of these toys you play with and whether you play with them nicely or not. It's all there for you to explore, and it's all the same to the universe which bits you pick. So, if that's the case, why do you bother with the bad stuff? The following pages are all about changing that shit up. For good.

Get out your abundance mentality, your feelings of gratitude, your beliefs, your dreams, and your spiritual framework. These are your All-Zones Access Pass to the universe. You're ready to let yourself loose.

LIGHTEN UP

In the spirit of fun, my friend Georgia and I snuck up to the North Coast of New South Wales for a weekend escape. Escaping our physical surroundings was a no-brainer, especially for two business architects who use masculine energy to organise every minute of their scheduled lives. Set date, book flight, order taxi, get on plane. Easy. But how to escape the self? My self is clingy. She wants to follow me everywhere I go even when I tell her she is not invited because her limitations and judgements have no place where I'm going. She doesn't take it well. While I packed, my self sat in a corner feeling abandoned, worrying that I might never come home. It was so hard to watch that I caved and let her come along. And she bloody sat on my lap the whole way there and then dominated the entire conversation once we arrived too. And then I felt disappointed that I had been weak by letting her come along. So solving this problem took some radical action.

I went down to the beach. It was a public beach, but it wasn't crowded. So I stripped off naked and went screaming into the ocean while my friend Georgia filmed me with her phone. My self was mortified. And guess what? I did not see her again for the whole weekend. Huzzah!

So this begged the question: "Why can't I be that fun person all the time?" And if you're imagining me turning up at the office naked and screaming, then you have missed the point. But you should totally head over to YouTube to see the actual footage that was taken that day of me in the nicky-noo-nar scuttling down the beach and into the surf . . . Jesus, no, just kidding, I'm not showing you that, not a chance. Not. A. Fucking. Chance. It got deleted.

Anyway, back to why I wasn't that fun person all the time. The answer: "Because you're a grown-up."

Sorry, what?

And there proceeded an internal argument between self Kate and fun Kate that went something like this:

"What does that even mean? Grown-up?"

"It means you take things seriously. If you're having fun all the time, people won't take you seriously, and especially at work, people need to know you are taking things seriously otherwise they won't think you're doing a good job, and if you don't do a good job then you won't get paid and then your family will starve and you'll all die."

"Christ. The drama. I'm just talking about livening it up a bit."

"Yeah, well, good luck with that. I don't know if you've noticed, but you work in a government office. The federal government is not known for its sense of humour."

"You're so boring."

"You're so unrealistic."

Okay, kids, settle down. I'm pretty pretty sure we can sort this out just by taking everything a bit less seriously, just like I did with my naked body. Streaking down a public beach was such a good start. I was determined to keep the momentum going with options that also involved clothes—I wanted variety, not to be a one-trick pony. So I read Chapter 2, dug deep into my swag bag, and looked inside myself for a bit to see what my feelings were telling me my next move should be. Your feelings along with your intuition, those internal urges and nudges, are always hovering in the background waiting for you to take notice of them. They have the guidance you need, in any moment, to make the right move. This includes how to have fun even in the most serious of situations, if that's what you want. Those feelings will tell you if that's what you want right now. If you feel like you want to be having more fun or are not enjoying being drab and serious, then that's your intuition telling you, yep, yep, more fun is needed here. And if you don't know how to go about it, then tune into the very next thing you feel like doing. It doesn't have to be a burning urge or some great blast of inspiration. Just a whisper of curiosity is all there is sometimes, and that's fine. Anything that points you in the direction of your attraction.

Your other self, your ego, the serious part of you that worries about what other people think, may well try to take over and tell you how dumb that idea is, how misaligned it is with the core objectives of the serious task at hand, so practise dialling down the ego tone and listening to your intuition even if you don't do anything about it to start with. When that ego-brain gets in the way and tells you all the reasons why you shouldn't do it, it's hard to ignore. You're so used to being bullied by that domineering two-dimensional slice of grey matter that, sometimes, watching your intuition unobtrusively for a bit is all that's possible for now. Fool ego-brain into thinking you're still its slave while fraternising illicitly with master intuition, and see what you learn. You'll discover in time that no matter how ludicrous or twisted or against the grain your intuition seems from ego-brain's perspective, when you finally act on it, you'll realise it was actually the most brilliant idea ever, and that ego-brain could never have thought of it in a million years.

Start somewhere where the stakes aren't very high, like at the beach on holidays. When you get the urge to go skinny dipping at the beach and your ego-brain is telling you the well-worn reasons why you should not, have a deeper look at the situation before you discount the idea completely. I realised that what was at stake was my embarrassment—not my survival, not the planet, not my bank account, or my kids. The beach was practically deserted, it was a laid-back community where being naked isn't such a big deal, so it was unlikely anybody was going to call the police or even get offended. If anything, the one or two people who saw us from a distance appeared to get a real kick out of our bizarre experiment. Perhaps the universe was gifting the image of my naked joy to them as a way of giving them permission to let loose too.

And don't let my example of having fun put you off discovering yours. Perhaps you were raised in a wild, hippie community where all you wanted to do was put on a business suit and never be seen naked again. Your idea of rebellion might be getting dressed in sensible heels and a collared shirt and going into the office for eight hours. That could be your idea of letting go. One of the biggest inhibitors to figuring out what you want is looking at what other people are enjoying and thinking that you should enjoy it too. Again, back to the buffet: Just because everybody else enjoys devilled eggs doesn't mean you have to.

When you look around the planet and see what appeals to you and what sparks your curiosity, the things that attract you and excite you, that's the universe guiding you. Think of those things as a psychic prediction. That feeling of positive attraction you feel toward something is because you're supposed to have it—it's the best fit for you. It's the universe's way of saying, "Here, check this out. It made me think of you. You're gonna love it." The universe puts things in your path that you love to encourage you to move in that direction, like a treasure hunt, because it knows the path you need to take to live your best life and to enhance the lives of others. So if you like it, it's for you. If you don't like it, then it's not. Classic game of hotter/colder. And you're not going to question the universe, are you? Universe knows best. Keep that in mind every time you find yourself saying, "But getting what I want is too hard" or "It's shunning my responsibilities" or "It's rude" or "I feel awkward" or any of those excuses that ego-brain makes, and bring it back to this moment, the now, and what the very next moment is drawing you to. Of everything you could do right now, which one appeals to you the most? This is the universe talking to you. It's about recognizing who you are at this very moment. It's about acknowledging the true you.

Here's a story of the crafty universe at work: I was once stuck in a taxi with somebody who had verbal diarrhoea. She was an extraverted thinker, and every single thing that occurred to her got said out loud, and it was driving me nuts. She started up a rant about getting a chicken out of the freezer when she got home, and then suddenly she would point urgently out the window and declare, "Church! Look! Look! And dog park!"

I was ready to set my face on fire. Keeping up was exhausting. She would ask me a question and halfway through my answer, there would be another exclamation, "Look! Look! Rabbit!"

Then, before I could finish answering her original question, she would start telling me a story—but a new interruption would inevitably happen when my attention was pulled out the window yet again to a camel with no humps, or whatever.

In that moment, my intuition was telling me to completely ignore her, I couldn't keep up (nor did I want to), but my social sensibility, my ego-brain, was telling me that was impossible, this was somebody I needed to show respect to, and ignoring her would be the epitome of impoliteness. But as a last resort, fueled by desperation, I gave myself permission to stop the nods and the oohs and aahs of acknowledgment, the feigning interest in what was being said, and the meaningless replies, and instead I allowed myself to stare out the window, viewing the humpless camel and the passing landscape on my own. I instantly calmed down, and, amazingly, so did she. She stopped talking altogether. I feel like not only was that the best outcome for me, but it also did her a big favour because it helped her calm her nervous system down in a way that wasn't possible while I was encouraging the conversation with my uh-huhs and oh reallys. She was probably as relieved as I was that there was finally silence. And quite possibly the taxi driver too. Who knows how far-reaching the effects of me doing what I felt was authentic for me in that moment had on the universe even though it had seemed so counterintuitive from my ego-brain's perspective.

There's a reason why I chose this particular story to tell. There's a nuance I want to point out. When you're in any adverse situation, you probably feel triggered and have many feelings and urges. When using your feelings as your guide, this is a reminder to choose the one that comes from the highest intention. My urge to lash out and tell this woman to JUST SHUT THE FUCK UP was coming from a place of frustration and entrapment and was not going to lead to the feeling of peace that I craved. The desire to ignore her, however, came from a place of self-love. It felt like a gift to myself, a hug, the slipping of the escape key to my inner prisoner through the iron bars of my cell. My ego-brain also had to acknowledge that ignoring her would, indeed, bring me a sense of peace, and that the other, more hurtful, options would not.

FUN AT WORK

When I first started out in the workforce, I got a job at a call centre, and in one of my first training sessions, the very enthusiastic teacher finished the session with a flourish by saying, "Most importantly, don't forget to have fun!"

I took this recommendation very seriously. Each day, I made sure I was having fun so that I didn't disappoint management. All day, on every call, with every human interaction, with my colleagues, in the lunchroom, even as I was learning how to reboot my computer after it had crashed and lost a day's work, I was having some serious fun. As my career progressed, however, I would look around me and notice that other people in the office weren't having the same fun I was. I was starting to look like a bit of a freakshow. So I toned it down. And down. And down.

I have been told numerous times by management throughout the years to "make sure you have fun!" But these days, I realise, it's best taken without the exclamation mark. The same way somebody who is extremely caffeine-sensitive doesn't need cocaine. Even after all these years, I've never fully figured out what the government definition of fun is, but I have learned that it's not the same as mine. So I resigned myself to accept that work wasn't meant to be "my type of fun."

That was, until I met Georgia. Georgia and I aren't just nudie beach buddies, we also work together and have done for many years. There's a story from my childhood that epitomises my friendship with Georgia. I had a best friend in preschool, and her name was Tabby, and she was a lot like Georgia. Every afternoon, all the kids had to have a nap in a big room where there were rows of mats laid out on the floor. One of the teachers was helping me find a spare mat, and she took me over to one right next to Tabby. When Tabby and I saw that we were going to be napping next to each other, our eyes lit up with the mutual recognition that this was going to be the best naptime ever. On seeing our faces, the teacher instantly whisked me away and took me to another mat on the opposite side of the room next to Angus, who was already asleep. You put me and Georgia next to each other and nobody is going to be getting much sleep.

Georgia and I were tasked with running a series of workshops around the country. We started out being very serious and business-like. We would turn up at the office in each city with our starched collars and our sensible handbags, and we would introduce ourselves with our full names followed by our credentials. At the end of each day, Georgia and I would go back to the hotel and we'd debrief on the day's work and start planning the next session. We did most of our planning in the spa. Let's just take a long, silent pause here, and let that sink in. Come on, I mean, you know what happens in the spa: You relax, open up, and start seeing life in a different way. When you are Georgia and Kate trying not to be yourselves, the last thing you might want is to relax and see life differently. Running a conventional government workshop was hard enough without stimulating our expansive minds. But it was too late. The ideas started hitting us like a meteor shower. They would overtake us as if they were little aliens from outer space, controlling our brains with their stun guns, and we'd feel compelled to follow their lead. When we got back into the workshop the next day, we were fighting a force of creativity that was too hard to hold back. Workshops started getting really colourful, and I don't just mean using pink and purple whiteboard markers. By the end of the day, jackets were flung across the back of chairs, there was leftover focaccia and sushi rolls scattered across the table, and everybody was clamouring at the whiteboard trying to draw diagrams of their own subconscious.

After each trip, we would dutifully return to the Canberra office and submit our formal report and not say a word about what had really gone on.

But then one time, somebody in one of the workshops laughed so hard at something Georgia said, that chicken sandwich went flying across the boardroom table, and when we got back to head office, our manager asked why there was meat all over his report, and we finally had to fess up. There was a serious pause after which he replied, "Yeah, we already know. We've been getting calls about it. They're calling it the Kate and Georgia Show. Now everybody is trying to book tickets. The thing you should be sorry for is that we don't have the budget to please them all."

What? It was just like those scenes in formulaic movies where the hero finally drums up the courage to come out of the closet only to discover that everybody already knows he's gay, and no one cares.

It could be easy to lament that I had wasted so much time and effort trying not to have fun. But was it really wasted? Because sometimes, the best way to learn who you really are is to first discover who you're not. Nothing in life is wasted. It's all reusable. The universe is good like that.

The words "work" and "play" are often used in the same sentence to highlight the separation between the two, but consider what a sense of playfulness does for feelings of satisfaction and commitment. Having more fun at work leads to greater engagement, which ultimately improves work performance and dedication to the organisation where you work. Taking your work seriously is different from being serious. Work, like any activity you undertake, is an opportunity to explore and discover yourself. Are you prone to being too serious to your own detriment? I am. To lighten it up a bit, I imagine my office is a film set and I am an actor playing the role of a business architect. I've got to play the role as convincingly as possible because I'm a good actor, but underneath, I know it's just a role. The real me is in the fun and the exploration. Oh, and the fact that I'm getting paid to have this much fun. Being authentic is not limited to one part of your life or the part of your life you feel most comfortable showing up in. It applies to everything you do, all the roles you play, especially the high-stakes ones, like work.

DESIGN YOUR IDEAL LIFE

So back to the North Coast. Georgia and I were on a roll after the swim as our new, braver selves. We wondered what it would be like to be living the highest version of ourselves all the time. The weather was beautiful, there was nowhere we had to be, and there was no better time to start using our imaginations to really get into the vibe of the women we were to become, so we wandered up the beach along the boardwalk when, suddenly, as we turned a corner, the aroma of herbs, spices, and wood-smoked fire hit us, and there in front of us was a restaurant. It lured us in. We sat under the tree canopy and ordered shared plates and drinks, and we were no longer Kate and Georgia on a weekend away from Canberra, we were Kate and Georgia in Monte Carlo, halfway through a round-the-world tour talking to people about living their dream lives. We are very fun and entertaining women who have brought their pink and purple pens. Everywhere we go, people pick up on our vibe. The waiter who came to take our order felt this, so he too was very entertaining and pleasant and provided excellent service, which just made us happier, and that vibe radiated throughout the entire restaurant so that everybody there was having a wonderful time.

Invest some time and creativity into designing your perfect life. Take yourself somewhere you can imagine your future self being once you are that amazing entrepreneur, physicist, YouTuber, snowboarder, mother, scuba diver, speaker, philanthropist, fun-loving goddess, or whatever you want to become, and get stuck into imagining a no-holds-barred version of your ideal life.

Use your free-form desires from the dreaming chapter to have fun conjuring up your perfect life. It's an exercise where limitations get left at the door. Even the physical laws of the universe are optional. But what matters most is that for every single thing you desire for your life, for every million dollars, every Tesla, every frizz perm, every uninterrupted hour of leisure time—whatever it is you want—you have to also specify how you want it to make you feel. This is very important. What is your emotional relationship with this new thing or situation or person going to be? Until you know how you want to feel in your ideal life, it can be hard to come to any firm conclusions about what is the best life for you. I know that is really hard to believe. Many of you might know without a doubt that ten million dollars would make your life perfect and that's all you need to know, but if you go ask your local neighbourhood billionaire whether a billion dollars has taken away all the hangups and issues that keep her awake at night,

I can assure you the answer will be *no*. And, in actual fact, she might even give you, free of charge, the insight that having a billion dollars has revealed a whole bunch of new issues that she didn't even know existed before she got rich.

This game is good for practising how to not judge yourself for all the things you want because your aim is to really rack up an enormous bill. The universe is paying. It's infinite and abundant, remember? If you have a voice in your head saying, "I can't believe you actually want that" or "Haven't you had enough already?" then isn't that just a fantastic opportunity to do some digging into your underlying beliefs about why you don't think you should have everything you want?

It's also important not to get caught up in how you will get this perfect life. That's the universe's job. This is a game of imagination, not a logistics project. The How Vortex is where dreams go to die. Instead, imagine that your life is already like this. Present tense. It doesn't matter how it happened anymore because it already has.

Put yourself somewhere beautiful, where you feel like you're already living your perfect life, and start designing. The more you flex your imagination, your "anything is possible" mentality, and your storytelling prowess, the more you'll tune in with what's really possible, what you really want, and how you want to feel. When you merge what you want with how you want it to feel, then you're bringing your imagination and your heart closer. Typically, those two live rather separate lives. What you think you want and what you actually need in order to be happy can be quite different, and it's hard to see that there is even a gap. The aim is to bring those two closer together with your feelings.

Now, I recognise that using the word "perfect" might be counter-productive in this context. I'm describing this exercise as something you might do for fun, but if you're somebody who takes your gaming seriously, then let's have a chat about perfectionism. You can ask me anything you want about perfectionism, and I can talk to you about it, and I suspect many of you are the same. I chased that elusive diva for years. Still do sometimes. I've been warned against it, told it's a fruitless exercise, that perfection is the enemy of good, to which I usually reply, "I don't want good. I've been good all my life. I want fucking majestic."

But perfectionism doesn't return calls. She's got standards that change with the wind, and her response to you finally delivering something perfect is to point out all the other times where you didn't and probably never will after this.

So if you find yourself playing this game and being dissatisfied with the outcome because you're not sure if what you can think of is really perfect enough for you, then congratulations, you have just reached an advanced conclusion that will put you a step ahead when I talk about manifesting in the next section. The reality is that your idea of perfect includes the concept of flawless, but a flawless life is far from a perfect one because, for starters, it would be boring as fuck. So don't worry about this apparent contradiction. There is an answer for it in the next section, and it's brilliant.

For everyone else who enjoyed playing the game and was able to describe their perfect life without any stress, congrats to you too because you figured out how to just have fun and not get all in your head about it.

So play this game as much as you like, whoever you are. Practise until you are at a semi-professional level because it's going to be really useful in the next section. Play any time you're in a situation that reflects the person you want to be, whether it's somewhere posh having a cocktail, eating loaded fries at a footy game, or having a hot bath by yourself. Wherever it is that you are, be that new person. Time starts now.

MANIFESTING

I feel like this section needs a backing track, like something upbeat with heavy bass that gets the audience all revved up, so by the time the hyper Tony Robbins-style emcee comes on stage, everybody is out of their seats and waving their hands in the air. And because you've trained your imagination so well by now, all it takes is a little bit of zest from Spotify and you can have all that in your own living room and you can start learning about MANIFESTING!

I get excited about manifesting because it's how you really can consciously create a life you love. What's not to get excited about? Hopefully by now you've realised just how much of your own reality you have the power to create, so manifesting needn't be a magical thought process that's exclusive to mystics and weirdos. And you don't need to believe in a higher consciousness to do it. You're unconsciously manifesting all the time—your beliefs and your feelings become things—so manifesting in this context is about understanding how this process works and leveraging it to get the very best out of yourself and of life.

Manifesting is all about the vibrational frequency of your emotions. These work like a magnet to attract things into your life that are a vibrational match for your emotions. It's how everything in your life, the good and the bad, has evolved. So, to get you started, don't focus on the chaos you've been unconsciously manifesting, just focus on the stuff you already have and love and the things you really desire. The best use of manifesting is to bring about the things you do want rather than try to eliminate those you don't. If you engage a builder to build you a house and you say, "I don't want a single storey brick house anymore," you're not nearly as likely to get your dream home as you are if you start with, "Build me a stone castle with pointy turrets and a swimmable moat."

The best bit about manifesting is that the process in itself feels divine, regardless of the outcome. And that's the point—manifesting is designed to make you feel good in the here and now, and that, in turn, is what manifests more. If you're somebody who has tried meditation but can't quite get into it because you get bored with your own breathing, or you haven't got the patience to stay the distance, then manifesting could also act as a good alternative because, while it still requires focus, you get to pick what you focus on, and you don't have to sit still while you do it. You get to concentrate on feel-good feelings rather than just the back of your own eyelids.

To start manifesting, use the Cultivating New Feelings exercise that you blissed out on in Chapter 2 to tune into the vibrational frequency that matches the way you want to feel about the things you want to attract into your life. Gratitude (the colour, the emotion, but not the list) is an excellent starting point for manifesting. Every time you feel gratitude for anything you have in your life, it's like saying to the universe, "I love feeling this way. Bring me more things that make me feel like this. Fill my life to the brim with this."

Some of you might be able to summon the feeling of gratitude as an isolated feeling, but some of you might need to focus on the thing for which you are grateful before you can feel the gratitude. A lot of the advice about manifesting talks about focussing on the thing you want to manifest and how you think it will make you feel. Placing your focus on a tangible object or situation is the only way some people can summon their gratitude. If this is you, then use the object of your focus as the launching pad for gratitude rather than the expectation that getting it is the only way to succeed. Said another way, don't get too attached to the thing you want. The universe, a.k.a. God, Nature, All That Is, the spiritual belief framework you created for yourself in the last chapter, is the highest, wisest version of you, and it has access to all the knowledge that you don't, and it has ideas about what you really, really want that you can't think of yet, so you don't have to be too specific about the tangible things you want because the universe will sort that out for you. It knows better than you, and it knows what other goodies are out there that you don't. It's got your back, and even though you are its creator, it's also yours, and it's smarter than you in every way. Accept that it just is.

Also, specifying exactly what you want is limiting. I mean, if you really, really want something and you can't let it go, then by all means order it from the universe. It won't do you any harm. You just forfeit the delight and surprise of receiving a present more perfect than you could ever imagine. Because when you let the universe loose in the shopping mall of your life with an unlimited budget, you get nothing less than divine creation in return.

Speaking of budgets, manifesting is no place for limitations, financial or other. Define your life by what you desire, not by what you can afford. Have a quick look at your life now and see if you can identify how much of what you want is actually constrained by what you can afford or what you think is possible for you. Thinking like this for too long will lead you to believe that the lesser, more affordable version is all you want.

So place your order with your gratitude and your mindset of abundance and fuel it with your imagination. Use your everyday life to find anything that makes you feel gratitude and love and bliss and any of the feel-goods. And then sit back, relax, and focus on the knowing (and more gratitude) that it is on its way. Just like when you order your food at a restaurant, you don't know exactly when it will arrive, but you trust that it will, and you don't have to do anything other than chill out and chat with your friends, knowing that your food will come when it's cooked to perfection. Also, one of the best bits about not knowing exactly when your order will arrive is that the universe, because it's the universe and it knows everything about everything that's going on, knows the best delivery timeframe to suit you. You could never in a million years predict the timing for something as well as the universe can. You think you know, and often when you're desperate and impatient or have a deadline, that thing on the buffet looks so good that you simply must have it NOW even though you're already full. Or else you think that someone else might get it before you, so you better take it in case. All symptoms of lack, which only serve to push your order further away. It's going to arrive when it arrives, and it will come when you're ready, not just when you think you're ready.

You also don't know how it will come to you. If you try to execute how you're going to get it, then you're limiting yourself to what you think is possible. Yawn. The most creative, exciting part of this whole deal is in the how, and it's particularly fun when there's something that you desire and you can't possibly figure out how you could get it. All you can do is trust that the solution exists and that the universe will deliver. And then you get to be blown away when it does and you finally see how it was done. It's like seeing a magic trick—a really, really good one.

This trust is critical. If you don't have a faith or belief in a higher power, or even if you do, you might not be well versed with putting your trust in something other than your own cognitive and physical ability. I invite you to give this a go even if you are sceptical, and play around with the feeling of trust, the vibrational frequency of knowing your needs are being attended to for your highest good, and see how that feels. Have some fun with it. This is, after all, a chapter on play.

So get this for one of my all-time sweetest manifesting stories: There was a time when I had an obligatory work party to go to, but I really didn't want to attend because it was in the middle of summer, and I knew it was going to be a stinking hot day. It was at an outdoor venue, and I felt self-conscious about having bare legs in front of my work crowd (I know, right? Says Miss Nude Beach 2022). But I didn't want to have pants on or a long skirt either because it would be too hot. So I went shopping, and I was trying to find an outfit that would keep me cool but also keep me covered. I didn't know if such a thing existed, and, not surprisingly, I couldn't find anything. So I handed this problem over to the universe. I got myself into a nice outdoor situation where I could easily imagine myself feeling cool and comfortable in what I was wearing. I didn't leave it at that; I also visualised feeling amazing and confident and beautiful in what I was wearing. I went all out for this visualisation, I tell you, and I felt I had nailed it with a pure, unwavering vibration that would have me feeling confident, attractive-but-not-too-wenchy, and physically comfortable. I couldn't figure out what sort of outfit could possibly fit all those criteria because I felt I had thought of everything, and I knew what fashions were out there. I knew there were jumpsuits, kaftans, mumus, capri pants, long flowing linen skirts, like, how many other things could there possibly be? Toga? Sarong? None of those was suitable. So I put my trust in the universe. And I said, "Look, can you solve this problem, please? I just need to feel good without looking like a glow worm."

Do you want to know how the universe solved the problem? The party was cancelled. Ha! Now there's a solution that I didn't think of, and even if I had, I couldn't have executed it myself because I wasn't in charge. I wanted to not go to the party so much more than I wanted a new outfit. How freaking funny, yeah? The universe is hilarious as well as creative.

If you're feeling a bit sceptical about manifesting, revisit your beliefs and see whether you can shift to a more abundant, open mindset before you start. Start with something small. Start with manifesting an hour to yourself or a dolphin sighting, or anything you're interested in. Keep it small and take your time. Get into that lovely feeling you get when you're gifted with a pleasant surprise that has you saying, "Oh wow! I love it! Thank you!"

And make sure you tell yourself how awesome you are when it happens. It's easy to manifest something amazing and then move on thirty seconds later without recognizing the magical part you played in attracting whatever it was into your life. There are many different ways to conceptualise manifesting. I could go on forever about it, so if you're interested in doing more, my website has a video you can watch to discover different ways to slice, dice, carve, stew, taste, sip, and dip into manifesting to change your life.

TAKE ACTION

Using your gratitude and your desires is the feminine-energy component to manifesting, allowing you to get into the vibration of who you want to be and what you want in your life. It's your vision. The masculine-energy component is where you take action that is aligned with your vision. And this is just as fun as creating the vision because once you are in the same frequency as your vision, the life it holds is already on its way, so you'd better prepare yourself for its arrival. One way to decide which action to take is to imagine that, without a doubt, you will be receiving what you have ordered. Are you prepared for it? Are you the person you need to be in order to live with it, to savour it, to deal with this change? What might you need to do, learn, or know first so that you will recognise it when it comes and be able to accommodate it seamlessly into your life?

If you want that promotion, do you have the knowledge you need to do the job and the availability for more responsibility? Can your nervous system deal with the pressure? Do you have the outfits you need to wear for it? All of these require action before you can happily receive what you have wished for, and these actions also help you stay in alignment with your dreams while you get there, i.e., until you realise that you already are there and were all along.

I wanted to manifest an in-ground swimming pool in my backyard. Last spring, the coming summer was predicted to be a hot one. I love to swim, and on hot days, I need to cool off at least ten times a day. I also love the look of water and love having a sizable body of it near me at all times. So, once the idea of a pool occurred to me, I was desperate to have it as soon as I could. But I'd never owned a swimming pool. I didn't know what it actually felt like or what was involved. So, to prepare myself and to kickstart my manifestation, I started looking at swimming pools and getting a feel for what I liked. I investigated where in the yard it could go and what type of decking I wanted around it so that I could more easily visualise it. Most importantly, I needed to know what it would feel like to actually go for a swim every morning, so I bought a $150 above-ground, thigh-deep kids pool that I set up in the backyard. No laughing. It really worked for me because, every morning, I've been able to stretch out in it and get my head under and gradually cultivate the feeling of joy that I get from being able to swim anytime I please. It also taught me what is involved in cleaning it, chlorinating it, and maintaining it, and a whole load of other realisations about what it's like to have a pool. Several months on, I am a lot clearer on what I need to be prepared for when the bigger pool comes.

I still don't have the in-ground swimming pool. People who visit our house are still walking into the backyard, looking at the pool and saying, "I thought your kids were almost grown up?" to which I reply, a bit sheepishly, "It's mine. It's a manifesting tool." But in a strange twist, the current setup meets all my needs. The urgency for the bigger pool that I felt at the beginning of the summer has been removed, and that's a really important step because the vibration of urgency is counterproductive to manifesting. Urgency is a feeling of lack, a vibration of not having rather than having, so it sends a message out to the universe that you want to feel more urgency. The feeling of wanting works in the same way. Wanting is also a feeling of lack. If you focus on how much you want something, then "wanting" becomes the message that gets sent out to the universe and the universe says, "Okay, more wanting and no having, coming right up." Replace the feeling of "want" with "desire" because desire is about receiving pleasure from something if it arrives without being dependent on it for your own happiness. Wanting is more desperate, and you know from watching rom-coms that this is not an ideal headspace to be in when you're looking to attract love.

Looking back on my original request to the universe for the pool, all my criteria have actually been met by the above-ground kids pool, so as far as the universe is concerned, perhaps this transaction is complete. The action I took not only prepared me for what was involved in having a permanent backyard pool, but it also showed me what was important and what I really needed versus what I thought I wanted. It has also gotten me so much closer to the genuine feeling of gratitude I have for being able to cool off on demand—that gratitude being the essential ingredient for manifestation and which I found hard to cultivate before I had the little pool.

My next step is to manifest an aesthetically pleasing pool. And yeah, I know, I'm going to want to address my negative feelings and beliefs about why the kids pool, which gives me so much joy and meets all my needs, isn't enough. Taking aligned action gives you the chance to tweak your desires as you go, and it teaches you about what you really want. And by "aligned," I mean making sure that as you undertake the action, you feel the same emotion as the emotion that motivated it. It also means you don't have to wait until the life you want is delivered before you actually start living it.

Taking action bridges the gap between vision and reality. Action turns thoughts into tangible outcomes, and without it, dreams and manifestations remain abstract. Taking action is how you let the universe know that you are serious about your dreams. It's about changing your life and announcing that you are willing to do the work to get there. Even the smallest action in the direction of your dreams is a gesture of openness and resilience, and as you know, where your focus goes, energy flows. Action directs your focus.

RECEIVING

One Christmas when I was very little, maybe around three years old, I received a toy that was better than anything I had ever seen (small kids are amazing manifestors—after all, they believe in Santa with all their hearts). It was a little red house with a yellow roof that you could pull apart into pieces like a puzzle and rebuild. Once built, you could stick different shapes through little holes in the roof and hear them clunk to the bottom, then you could dismantle the house, pull the pieces out, rebuild, and start posting all over again. It was my absolute dream. As I was tearing the parts out of the packaging, my brother came over and said, "Wow, that looks great! Can I have a turn?" He was a bit older than me, so he was beyond wanting to post things into little plastic boxes and hear them go clunk, but I had already been lectured about how sharing makes you a good person and that giving is better than receiving. Throw into the mix that I was desperate for my brother's approval, and I handed the toy over to him before I'd even tried it out myself. Within thirty seconds, he had broken it beyond repair.

Now don't worry too much about him or me in this circumstance because I got him back a few years later by accidentally killing his pet mouse, but the point of this story is that giving only works when you've already received and when you feel like you've got enough. If you're giving by obligation, from a deficit, or with the hope of getting something in return, then it's being done with an insincere intention. The antidote to this is to learn to receive with all your heart first. Before you can be a good giver, you need to be a good receiver. Imagine putting someone else's oxygen mask on in a crashing plane when you haven't got your mask on yet. We're always given this advice and it's pretty profound. Picture what it's like when you're gasping for air while the reluctant passenger next to you is thrashing about as you try to stick a mask on them. It doesn't make much sense.

Before you can be a good manifestor, you need to be able to receive what you've ordered from the universe. With all your heart and with immense gratitude. It's easy enough to say, "Ooh, gosh, I like that. I want that." But it's a little harder when it all turns up in an enormous delivery van and starts getting unloaded in your driveway, and all your neighbours are watching as you say to the delivery man, "Yep, I ordered that, and I also ordered that and that and that, and I also liked that, so I got that too."

Now there's a hell of a lot in your driveway, but as more and more people wander out of their homes with curiosity to watch the delivery, you start to question yourself. You might find yourself buying into your neighbours' judgement, which comes entirely from a place of lack.

So prepare yourself to receive. Get really good at it. People often don't think about this much because in many cultures, giving is the holy grail of goodliness. But receiving is an essential skill that makes the whole equation work. Start practising with a compliment. How hard is that for many people? Make sure you manifest the compliment you want, a compliment that you believe. Make your hair look amazing one morning, and wait for people to say that your hair looks amazing. Or bring a state-of-the-art salad to work and proudly sit in the lunchroom and eat it for all to see and weep. Keep the compliment little and manageable. Don't forget that young woman who almost starved to death because she couldn't receive some macaroni and cheese even though she had manifested it to her doorstep. Receiving is feminine energy all over. So embrace that feminine side of you, you too, guys, and learn how to receive everything you desire with the uninhibited excitement and gratitude of a big, licky puppy.

PERMISSION AND THE POWER YES

Can I just have another quick rant about the word *no*? As a toddler, when *no* was the only word I could say, it was my favourite word, and I used it liberally. I would say it to my parents, to my brother, to the neighbours, and to strangers in the street. I'd say it to my breakfast bowl, to the bathtub, and to the front door. Life was all one big gleeful *no*. Despite learning other words, I was so in the habit of saying *no* that I said it even when I meant *yes*. And I think that might have persisted into adulthood. I don't think I'm the only one with this affliction either. As an adult, you can get really trigger-happy with your use of the word *no*, mainly when it comes to saying it to yourself. And yet, in complete contrast, you've become strangely flaccid when it comes to putting your foot down and saying it to others. Have you noticed that? So weird.

Remember that small, dank hideout that you built around yourself with your beliefs? The walls and the roof of that place are made of *nos*. Thousands upon thousands of heavy-duty *nos* all cemented together to keep you in and the light out. And I don't know whether you've ever been inside somebody else's *no*-house, but it smells and the acoustics are bad. No matter what anybody says inside a *no*-house, it all reverberates with a "nooo" sound. It's like having a discordant choir of naysayers warbling inside your head.

It's time to rein in your habitual mouthing off of *no* and start saying *yes* to the things that are going to make your life worthwhile and exciting and enjoyable and meaningful and authentic, not just to the things that ensure your survival. You're here to do more than just get to the end of your life and be able to proudly declare, "I kept my head above water!"

Amazing things happen when you start saying *yes* to yourself, when you give yourself permission to do and have the things you love, just because. You start to cultivate courage, to take your power back, to stand up for yourself in front of yourself, and say, "Yes, I deserve this." Everybody deserves to be able to say *yes* to the things that reflect who they really are. The *yes* that you say to yourself when it's something you truly desire is real gratitude, it's real self-love. Nobody else is telling you what you should be grateful for or what you should love. You know what it is and you give it to yourself. That's double doses of gratitude. Receiving from yourself is unconditional love, an opportunity for you to say, "Here, this is for you!" and you can reply, "Oh, thank you so much! That's exactly what I wanted!"

Up the quota of *yesses* to yourself and make the *nos* the empowering type of *nos* that enforce the boundaries that allow you to be your authentic self.

Come visit a yes showroom to inspire the design of your own yes-house. From the front door of a yes-house, you are drawn into an enormous high-ceilinged space awash with light that streams in from floor-to-ceiling windows opening onto a huge balcony that overlooks the rainforest. Vines with enormous leaves grow from tall ceramic pots against the walls, and you can hear water trickling from an unseen fountain. Any words spoken in the yes-house sound beautiful and melodic, they echo in harmonies with "ommms" and "ahhhs" that make the trees sway and the flowers bloom and entice tropical birds to come land on the balcony and drop a few multicoloured feathers for you to put in your swag bag. Even the bird calls sound like "ooh yeah."

Saying yes to yourself requires no justification beyond "Because it feels good." If you're looking for reasons to say no to yourself, you will always find them. Always. But the most beautiful things in life are the ones that have no reason, they just are, and you do them just because. That's feminine energy, and the feminine does not exist for an outcome or a reason. She is not goal-oriented. She just is. When too many things in your life are goal-focussed, you get out of balance. So don't bother justifying yourself to the goddess, she's not interested in excuses, she just wants you there. Yes. Yes she does.

Insert a playful mindset into everything you do. Leave space in yourself to simultaneously experience what is currently in front of you and what it could be. Playing is a form of unleashing, of free-form discovery and doing something just because it feels good. Sounds like the definition of authenticity, doesn't it? It is.

CHAPTER 8

CELEBRATE

I t's time for the IT project after-party! You have reached a major milestone, and there is no going back. In IT, just like in life, there is never actually an end point, there is always more to build and bigger improvements to be made, and that's the important reason why you have to celebrate your efforts and your achievements as you go. And on the subject of build, did you notice there's no "construct" chapter in this book? You might be thinking, "When do I do the thing I need to do to be my authentic self?" That's the magic voodoo I did on you to get you moving toward your higher self without you noticing. In life, the design and build stages are also the planning stage and the end game. It's all just one big ongoing exploration with no finish line. Every moment you spend consciously aware of how you are being in the now is you being authentic. So, regardless of where you are in the journey, the universe says, "You already are and always were there, so please come to my party."

You know work parties aren't all jumping up and down to the music with your shirt off. There are always some people sitting in twos and threes reflecting on what has just been. Some are already hooking up because they collaborated so well in the office, they're keen to know how that goes without the ties and the cufflinks. Others are standing in larger groups at the bar loudly speculating on who's going to shag who tonight, and others are sitting on their own with a drink in their hand, observing the entire scene with quiet detachment.

You can celebrate your achievements and your growth in any way you like. It's about reflection, recognition, and release, in any format, so this party chapter offers a range of party games to make sure there is something for everyone.

COME AS YOU ARE

Have you ever been to a Come as You Are party? It's where you are called up by the host and asked what you are wearing (ooh, saucy), and once you've told them, you are invited to a party where that's how you have to show up. In life, sometimes you have to be fine with turning up in your shower cap and your knickers if that's what the situation requires.

By virtue of the fact that you are here now, you are complete, and you are ready for the party. There is nothing you need first before you embark on your journey to greater happiness and spiritual connection. There is no one you need to become, nobody you need to discuss it with, no plans you need to make. The gun has already gone off, and you are already in the race. No "just let me think about it," no "hold on, I have to fix this first" or "maybe when the kids are older" or "when I've paid off my mortgage." Everything you have done and accumulated so far is part of the trip, and you're bringing it all along with you, including (especially) any feelings of hesitation and unpreparedness.

Everything you are now, and anything you think you aren't yet, has a purpose. Nothing is wasted, not that failed investment, not your divorce, not that text message that you accidentally sent to the wrong person. It's all part of where you're going. It's got a role to play, so it comes along. There is nothing to fix and nothing to solve, those issues are all part of the swag bag. They're your map, remember? You don't want to leave them behind. Go rage about it in the other room for a bit if you want to. I've heard all the excuses. I've said them all myself. Still do on occasion. But they're all fear talking, and nothing else. They're definitely not one of those hot n' spicy clues from the universe telling you where your treasure is. If you stay right where you are and you do nothing and you feel no different, then the other side of your life will remain enticingly but annoyingly out of view.

Meanwhile, your soul and the universe are having a blast regardless of what you do. While you're trudging to work in the snow, snarling and bitter about yet another day at the office, your soul and the universe are sitting up top with their sunnies on and the wind in their hair, loving every minute of the crisp fresh air and the steady rhythm in your step. They're even enjoying the song that's playing out of a nearby store. It's your favourite, and you haven't noticed because you're too bummed about your situation, but you are walking in time to the beat without even knowing it. The universe reckons that's hysterical. Just to see if it can snap you out of your funk, it plays another song you love, this time on a car radio waiting at the traffic lights, but you're in way too deep. It tries again, it's having a bit of fun now, poking you to see when you'll flinch. This time, it sends you an old flame from university, walking toward you from the opposite direction. He looks at you and instantly recognises you, thinking, "Holy shit, she's still looking good." He stands up straighter and sucks in his gut then tries to catch your eye, hoping you'll remember him. But you're now so far away in your head that you almost walk into a lamppost, and not him. And so goes the game of the universe, trying to entice you into playing with it, to get you to notice it, and it will keep doing so for as long as it takes. Whenever you're interested in finally lifting your head up and opening your eyes, the clues will be there for you to follow. Each clue is like a treat in itself, like a chocolate wrapped in a wrapper with instructions to the next destination printed on the inside. And you also get the chocolate all to yourself.

So you have a choice to join your soul up on the viewing platform of your life or to stay down in the engine room with your human. The engine room is somewhere you might go as a quick side trip for interest, but that's it—it's not why you've come on the journey. It's like booking a cruise and staying in your windowless cabin for the whole trip. Stop saying, "I'm too busy being a prisoner to enjoy the path to freedom." Exactly when is a better time to set yourself free than now?

One of my favourite podcasters says, "Earth is where souls come for rapid expansion," meaning, there will never be a time where you aren't experiencing some kind of adversity. That's not the deal you signed up for when you chose this life. There is no magical destination that you are heading toward where all your problems disappear. Behind every challenge is a new one that was obscured by the first. There's a reason for that. There's no escaping it. Not sure if that makes you feel better or worse. Perhaps swallow this at the same time, as the antidote: Keep moving forward because on the other side of your greatest fear is your biggest achievement. There. That should feel better.

You've got to make the first move. Nobody can do it for you. And if you don't know what the first move should be, come and join me and the community via my website, kateangel.com, and you'll find out pretty bloody quickly.

TREASURE HUNT

In my twenties, I went on a date with a guy who told me that he remembers sitting in front of the fire at the age of five, contemplating the meaning of life. The first thing I thought when he said that was, "Well, we won't be going on a second date. You are way, way out of my league." I had delusionally thought that I could tell him I liked to ride horses and he would be really impressed. What I didn't ask him and wish I had was did he ever come up with the answer? Because I've now got it, and if he's been struggling with this question for the last thirty years, I can finally give him some peace.

I alluded to it in Chapters 1 and 2, and it'll make even more sense now that you've reached this point. I believe the purpose of life is to discover who you really are. Just let that one sit for a bit. I didn't make this up, by the way. It's an actual thing. Inside, you already have the answers to everything you need in life. You know what your gifts are, the things that you love that give you so much joy and the things that are going to give other people joy. Maybe you can't remember what a lot of them are because that discovery is what life is all about.

Imagine you are the universe, you are All That Is—technically, you actually are, but you don't remember—so, for now, imagine. As the universe, you know everything that is going to happen, you know everything that has happened, you know everything about yourself because you are All That Is. There can't be anything you don't know, otherwise you wouldn't be All That Is. So what is an all-knowing consciousness like that going to do with itself? It's going to play a game. Specifically, it's going to go on a treasure hunt on planet Earth. Human life is like a treasure hunt. All That Is created a bunch of souls, you included, and pinched them off from itself so that they're still connected, but they can't remember everything anymore. So you're still connected to All That Is even though you don't always know it, and All That Is gets to experience the discovery of itself vicariously through you. This same connection is also how you access the infinite knowledge and wisdom and insight you need to discover your treasures, which is you living vicariously through the universe. Like mutual admiration. Obviously, All That Is doesn't tell you where the treasures are hidden or how many there are or what they look like—that would ruin the fun. That's why you have a choice. If you don't want to play, you don't have to. Ever been forced to go on a treasure hunt when you didn't want to? Me too. And it sucks. So having that freedom of choice is essential to the fun.

All you know is that you've got to start looking. But you don't have to just blindly wander around the planet hoping to bump into something that looks like treasure. Luckily, you've been given a map and a compass. Your emotions are your compass that tell you whether you're heading in the right direction, and the pain and adversity you experience on your journey are the map. It's a topographic map with canyons and mountains, roadblocks, and hairy bends that, on first encounter, might be too hard to navigate, so you decide to take the long way around to get to the treasure on the other side. But as you learn and grow and discover your gifts, you're able to tackle some of the trickier obstacles so that you can get to more treasures quicker and more creatively. Or you might choose to sit this game out and lie in a meadow and stare at the stars for eighty years. The universe is cool with all of it. It's not like it's got anywhere else to be.

Every time you discover something about yourself, you're rewarded with the joy of "Ah! Look what I did!" and the universe gets to experience the same joy, and so it expands and grows because that joy of rediscovery is new. It's something it could never have felt before you, the human, rediscovered who you are.

You get to keep the treasure you find. The universe isn't mean like the kids at school who would tell you there was treasure when there wasn't, or, there was a treasure, but they'd wait for you to find it and then they would steal it from you. You discover your gifts, and you get to keep them and to play with them in whatever capacity you choose. And, in doing so, the universe also discovers more about itself because the things you create by exploring your new gift is what creativity is, and that's how the universe expands and evolves.

So, just like in a video game where you accumulate health, supplies, powers, and the like, stop every once in a while and admire what's in your pack so you can realise just how far you have come. Unpack everything, give stuff a polish and some TLC, including the items right at the bottom that you had almost forgotten about, but which, at the time, you thought were the best things ever. And there you have it, the full circle into gratitude. By celebrating every new find, you're setting yourself up to discover even more. It's a constant manifesting and gratitude cycle.

PIÑATA

There was a time before this life where you knew you were the universe. There was no separation between your soul and All That Is. But then the time came to be born, and you had to squeeze All That Is into yourself, and you would have looked at that tiny little body and wondered, "How the fuck am I going to fit all this in there?" But you managed. It was a tight fit, but you did it. All of it. The great spiritualist Ram Dass said that dying was like taking off a tight shoe. It stands to reason then that living is like walking around in moon boots. It's the trade-off for being able to go further and do more than if you didn't have anything on your feet at all, but it's a bit uncomfortable all the same. So, given the fact that you have the entire universe tucked inside your seams, you're only going to add more pressure by holding in any part of it that you know wants to flow from you—those bits that all your life you've been told are way too much or that you've decided are inappropriate.

When I talk about this concept to my husband, I do it in the context of how much effort I've always had to put into containing my energy. "Kate must learn to control her exuberance" was printed on every report card I received throughout my entire schooling life. But my husband says that because he is naturally quiet, he can't relate to that concept. He has spent his adult life thinking he should be more exuberant, not less. The universe is all of these things, the quiet and the loud, so if you're somebody like my husband who has judged yourself for being reserved or introverted or not speaking up more, or for not making enough jokes, then that's the universe being contained as well. That serenity, that comfortable-in-your-own-space-and-in-your-own-company vibration, that authentic you, when allowed to express itself, is like throwing a soft, fleece blanket out into the universe to cover everybody with a sense of peace. But when you hold that in, it feels just as uncomfortable as it does for me when I feel like I want to laugh raucously but I'm not allowed to. Let your authentic light shine. Spill the candy from within, and let everybody enjoy what you're really made of.

Take the time to find out who you are and to celebrate each discovery as a real win. And don't worry if you don't come up with all the answers—there are infinite answers anyway, and they are all subject to change without notice. Besides, you have all the time in the universe to do the searching. Discovering who you truly are is the only real job there is.

SPOTLIGHT

The process of receiving what you manifested changes you, so, by the time it arrives, you can be someone different. The original person wanted the thing so badly, but the person who now has it is like, "Yeah, I did that, so?" This is a good thing, but it can make it easy to miss the critical role you play in creating your life.

Six months ago, I had written a novel, a work of fiction, but no matter how many times I rewrote the ending, I wasn't happy with it. I was in love with the main character (which was a bit naughty really because he is only twenty-two and I am married) and I also loved the story and wanted to see it come to fruition, but I realised I wasn't going to be able to get there without some help. I couldn't imagine what type of help I needed, seeing as I was the only one who knew each character intimately and which strings had to be tied up to draw the whole thing to a logical and satisfying conclusion, so I threw it out to the universe. Instead of trying to imagine the final plotline, I focussed on the satisfied feeling I would have of the book being complete and me being so smitten with the ending that I would giggle smugly every time I re-read it. I also wanted to enjoy the process with whomever was going to help me; I wanted to feel the connection with them and the creativity and collaboration. I also didn't want to be time-stressed with other work. I wanted to be able to savour the experience and for the book to be my number one priority without distractions. You might be noticing a pattern here that my demands from the universe are pretty elaborate. As they should be.

Fast-forward to now and that book has still not been touched. My natural conclusion is that the request I put into the universe is still gestating. It was a big bloody ask, after all, and these things take time, so that's probably it.

But then, here I am writing this book. It's the product of an amazing association with some of the most incredible people who I hadn't even met six months ago. I've taken time off work so that I can wake up every morning and plunge straight into writing, something I also couldn't have imagined possible six months ago. I've even committed to a launch date with my publisher, so it's as if I know what it feels like to see the book published even before it's happened. The universe has dropped the mother of all gifts at my feet, and I almost missed it because I was focussed on the other book. Long blink of realisation.

The universe clearly realised that if I was going to enjoy this process the way I said I wanted to, it would have to be with a different book. Who knew? And what's more, maybe this book only exists as a path to get me in alignment to finish the first book, and this is only the first stage of my original request, the rest still pending in the cosmic warehouse, along with the in-ground swimming pool. In fact, everything in life is just a pathway to something else because, and I keep forgetting this myself because I've typed the opposite numerous times and keep having to delete it, *there is no final destination*. Which must mean you're already there, and if you don't feel it, that just means you've looked away for a minute.

Celebrating what you have manifested allows you to acknowledge your progress and provides a tangible sense of achievement. This tangible sense of achievement creates a feedback loop because it reinforces the belief that you can manifest your dreams and serves as a reminder of your power to call forth your most authentic life.

Moral of the story: Keep your eyes open, but don't stare too hard.

DANCE PARTY

I'll give you something to celebrate, something that will stop you wasting time and energy. It'll give you a reason to finally stop trying to understand the things that don't make sense. Just like when you dance, you do, and you create things just for the sake of it . . . just because.

Humans love logic; things that make sense; and answers, absolutes, promises, guarantees, and predictability. They love logic and its byproducts so much that schools, university degrees, even the syllabi themselves are based on it. As are governments and sometimes even religions. The appetite for logic appears to be insatiable. If logic were a commodity, the demand for it would have increased exponentially over time. And just like any commodity, some suffer a severe shortage of logic, while others overconsume it, to the detriment of everyone. There are those who have logic but choose not to use it. Some people think that a lack of logic is the root of all problems. Some think it's the opposite. Those who don't have much logic believe that others are using logic against them, and that's unfair because they don't have the logic to fight back. The logic argument goes on and on and no amount of logic seems to be able to solve it.

All of that was just to say that you need to get out of your head. The need for everything to make sense before you make a move actually has the counter effect—it makes you stuck. Recognise the difference between a wholehearted interest in a problem as a hobby or pastime and the obsessive need for something to be proven right before you can relax. The more logic you throw at a situation, the slower you will travel, and the more stuck you will get. Trust me, I work in a government office where this gets scientifically proven on an hourly basis.

Celebrating ambiguity in life encourages an open-minded approach to growth and transformation. By embracing the unknown and the uncertainty, you become more willing to explore new ideas, fostering a space for more creative thinking. This can lead to breakthroughs and innovations that would not have been possible in a rigid universe. Developing a tolerance for ambiguity—coming to understand that ambiguity is a part of the design—is how you cultivate a culture of inconclusiveness in your personal life and in the community around you. Contradiction is the birthplace of creativity, the space between everything that makes sense and everything that doesn't.

If you can accept this, then you'll be able to use every contradiction as a hall pass—permission from the universe to live your fullest life, unapologetically. Living a life of abundance does not need to make sense, so stop feeling like you have to justify yourself. Looking for the logic in what makes you happy will only serve to hold you back and make you doubt yourself. When you let go of this, you'll stop asking others to justify themselves too, and you'll release everyone from the shackles of logic. Who cares why you're happy? You just are. Take it and run.

Or, in the case of this party, take it and dance.

CHAPTER 9

COMMUNE

FIND YOUR PEOPLE

B eing an amateur musician, a number of more experienced musicians have advised me over the years to play with other musicians as a way of staying motivated and finding enjoyment in playing. I've taken their advice and have always gotten so much out of it, so I find myself evangelistically telling every budding musician I come across to do the same.

In fact, my enthusiasm, not having social boundaries like the rest of me does, has since spread to everywhere and anything so that, these days, whenever I talk with somebody who has just taken up sausage making or who collects pine clippings as a hobby or whatever, I insist that they find a group of like-minded people to uplevel their enjoyment. I tend to go on about it until they say that they will. It can be quite bewildering for some, especially when they don't realise the only way to make me stop is just to say *yes*.

It's a no-brainer, then, that if you're on the path to discovering your authentic and spiritual self, find yourself some like-minded individuals to hang out with. In your day-to-day life, you're going to be surrounded by people who aren't on the same path as you, people who are used to you the way you've always been and they like it like that, so you will undoubtedly encounter some resistance when you start to change. There will be questions and comments and interpretations as to what people think is going on, and it's easy to allow these opinions and reactions to pull you out of alignment and hold you back.

Being distracted by people who don't want you to change will attract more of these types of people in your life. Remember, where focus goes, energy flows. It can be very hard to stay the course without some friendly, like-minded support. Friends who know you as the person that you're trying to be and who understand your zigzagged, circular, squiggly (anything but linear, basically) journey will also understand when you occasionally regress, veer off the road, or make a mess. And they know this because they too have drawn their own weird shapes in the dirt as they follow their path to their higher selves.

It's important to note that you will still get stuck in your old ways as you start living each moment as your more authentic self. I've been going circular for years: I will leave my job because I need something new, and then I will get bored and go back again. And then I will get bored and leave, and then I'll get bored and go back again. A friend of mine does it with men. She'll decide that that's it, she's not dating men who treat her badly anymore. And then she'll find a new man, and he'll treat her badly, and she'll leave. And then she'll say she'll never do it again. Jimmy Barnes did it with drugs, John Farnham did it with retirement; you get the drift. Everyone has their cycles; they're the sand in the bathing suit of life that you just have to keep rinsing out as you go, so when you're about to cave, it helps to have people around you who can either keep you focussed until you see reason or who can pick you up and pull your skirt back down over your undies if you don't.

At the retreat where I'm writing this book are a group of women who get that. I can have any style of meltdown I like because they've done exactly the same thing at some point or another in their lives, and they get it. The moment I burst into tears because I can't find the perfect synonym for casserole, they're not going to be staring at me in horror or fear wondering what the hell's wrong. In fact, when this happened, one of them just laughed and said, "Welcome to day three." Another sat and held space for me as I blubbered indecipherably about the inadequacy of the word soup, and someone else suggested that I go outside and scream into the canyon. It all worked, but the best part was feeling like I could have a meltdown in the first place in exactly the way I needed to have a meltdown, not the way I think I should daintily, politely have a meltdown, as I do when I'm with anybody else.

So come and join us so that you can showcase your unique path to self-discovery, the celebrations, the epiphanies, the tantrums, the lot, and give us the chance to practise witnessing somebody else's authenticity without being freaked out. Come and meet me via my website or on Instagram. I would love to get to know you. Find people where you live, join online communities, go on retreats, or take courses where you will be exposed to people who are aiming for the same thing as you. I really need you to do this. Communing is yet another mechanism by which you can discover yourself, but it also helps hold all the good work you've done together. Being part of a supportive community provides a framework for change through shared goals, collaborative efforts, and collective wisdom. And so much fun. This shared purpose will amplify your individual efforts, creating a stronger drive to persevere in your pursuits. Those of us waiting for you there need you to do this. If you're in any way remotely drawn to aim for the highest version of yourself, then perhaps consider that you have been given this challenge by a higher authority, and who are you to question the universe, to play small? You'll find that if you really say *yes* to all those things that your heart desires, that you will be supported in doing them even though you can't in a million years imagine how that's going to play out. But that's the magic of it all. That's the creativity. That's the feminine energy you want to tap into.

Get up and walk with your new sense of balance. Fall often because, contrary to old-school attitudes, falling and mistakes are not a ticket to shame and blame and guilt, they're the tools by which you grow. So sprinkle them liberally on each meal and savour the taste, eat with gratitude, and let your body and the divine do the rest.

FACE THE RIGHT DIRECTION

Finding the right people to hang out with and support you in your journey means looking in the right place for them. This probably sounds a bit obvious, but there's a saying that goes, "If you want something you've never had, you have to do something you've never done." Here's a very simple story about breaking your patterns to reveal new layers of your own life.

When I was in high school, every Monday morning at 9:00 a.m., we had an assembly. On these days, every student in the school needed to have arrived on campus on time, have their books prepared for the first class, then be seated in the assembly hall ready for the headmistress to arrive and talk us through the week. And because I come from a bloodline of proudly prompt people, I was always ready on time. But my friends did not have this same skill set, so I would stand in the locker room with my bag neatly stashed and my books ready to go and nag them until 9:03 when we would all do a last-minute dash and get to the assembly hall late. Finally, in year twelve, after six years of nagging, one of my friends said, "Why don't you just go down on your own? You're ready. We'll meet you there." And the penny dropped. All this time, I had been waiting for the people who weren't ready, not realising that in the assembly hall were already a whole bunch of ready kids. I had been waiting for someone else to come with me before I felt like I was able to go. And that's a reflection of so many of the things that I haven't done in my life because I thought I needed others to do it with me or to do it first. The message: Go when you are ready.

Every Monday morning through high school, I had been facing the wrong direction. Just ahead of me, already waiting in the assembly hall, were all the people doing the thing I wanted to be doing. So align yourself with your shiny beacon, set your compass, and off you fuck. It's as simple as that. And remember what I said about excuses? If you're looking for them, you will always find them, which is consoling if you don't want to be doing something. But if you do, then start seeing excuses as one more thing you can ignore. Pretty sneaky, eh? Every excuse that you ignore is an obstacle overcome, and behind your obstacles are your wildest dreams. Boom.

So I'm not going to ask "What are you waiting for?" because I don't want to know. Just meet me up ahead when you've taken that step. I would love to meet you and introduce you to my community. Commit to finding your true self and hang out with the rest of us cool, hip, like-minded individuals who are uplevelling humanity. We're not interested in why you can't or what you're waiting for. That's only worth talking about once you have already come so far beyond that point that we can laugh raucously about all the things you used to think were holding you back and how small they seem now that they are behind you.

Refer to your group often, whether it's checking in with your community on Facebook or speaking to them on Zoom, at a cafe, or going on retreats. But my recommendation is to get into the habit of doing it, and do it often, and take aligned action every single day.

PRACTISE EMOTION WITH OTHER PEOPLE

A boss of mine told me in a performance review that I was the type of person who thought things only needed to be said once. She didn't mean it in a good way. So, to honour her feedback and as you get to the end of your journey with me, there are a few things I would like to reiterate with you. They are things that are best practised with other people.

The first thing is to continue to use words that reflect your own truth and that are for the highest good of all. This does not mean blurting out whatever comes into your mind. With self-mastery, you may well find yourself talking less, not more, especially as you start to question why you have chosen to speak in the first place. At least, it did for me. Ninety percent of everything I used to say really wasn't necessary, including the things I felt obliged to say in reply to questions I really didn't want to answer but felt put on the spot. Practise not answering questions you don't want to answer. Have some generic responses available in your repertoire that you can whip out on demand without having to think about how you deflect.

Second, own your emotions and allow yourself to feel them to the fullest extent. Recognise that doing this alone is a completely different exercise to doing it in the presence of others, and both are needed. Doing this with all types of people is great practice to become a master.

The third thing is to practise dealing with other people's emotions and the emergence of their inner toddler by not becoming one yourself. When somebody is reacting like a child and you can engage with them without regressing thirty years (or more), you know you have become a fucking legend. If you can elegantly master reacting to other people's emotions without compromising your own authenticity, you put yourself so much further ahead of the majority of the human race, and so many of the greatest, seemingly unreachable things the world has to offer suddenly become possible for you.

Back when I worked in a call centre, I used to sit near what was known as the Trades Desk. The Trades Desk was where a group of tradesmen used to take calls from householders who needed trades help. One day, I heard Simon, one of the tradesmen, take a call from a woman who was clearly deeply distressed. As I listened on, it took Simon quite some time to calm her down before he could even assess what the problem was and what type of help she needed. When he finally got to the bottom of it, he discovered that her toilet had overflowed, and she needed a plumber. It was easy for him to not share her distress because, in his eyes, that was an excessive reaction to a very fixable problem, so this woman's distress didn't cause him distress. Simon was able to easily manage the call with compassion even though he couldn't relate to this woman's emotional reaction. This, in fact, did him a favour because it didn't trigger any emotions of his own, and he, therefore, wasn't having to deal with his own emotions as well as hers.

But then there are circumstances where somebody else's emotion hits you deeply, where you read your own story into the behaviour they are exhibiting, and you tell a story about yourself around it as well. This is where dealing with someone else's emotions gets harder because your emotions are also running high. When you can relate to the other person's reaction, it's easy to project yourself onto them and to make an assumption that they are feeling what you are feeling for the same reasons. This is particularly true with kids. When your children are upset about something, it's easy to identify heavily with your own story of a similar nature and to get overly distressed on their behalf, with the assumption that whatever's going on for them is as bad as what's going on for you.

Projection is a normal psychological defence mechanism that provides temporary relief for your emotional discomfort. It externalises the problem and provides some emotional distance, allowing you to feel as though you have some control over what's happening even though what's happening is happening to you and not to the other person.

There is nothing wrong with this, though. It's not a problem, and it doesn't need to be fixed. It's a human trait, and all you need is to be aware of how it plays out for you. Regularly reflecting on your own emotions allows you to identify and explore your patterns of projection. This awareness alone will help you a thousand-fold. Practice self-compassion and allow yourself to have your emotions, the good and the bad. Your emotions are there, they're meant to exist, you don't need to question them. Just let them come up and watch as they ebb and flow. And whatever you do, just keep that toilet clean.

IT'S GOT TO BE NOW AND ONLY NOW

You'll start to discover how quickly you can change and how quickly you are changing once you embrace the change. You'll wonder why you ever stayed the same for so long before even though you were always changing (you just weren't noticing). What has changed the most is your willingness to accept change, your conscious decision to change, and your celebration of your own evolution.

Most members of our species aren't big fans of change. They prefer things to be static from one moment to the next. They especially like people to be like that. When people comment that somebody has changed, it's often with a negative energy. They're feeling the road surface suddenly start to move beneath them because they can no longer predict the other person's behaviour using the same old formula. They feel unsteady without the consistency they're attached to. Their fear response is saying, "Ah, shit. Now I'm going to have to learn a brand new set of rules to figure you out."

This desire for predictability, for consistency, can often be hard for you as you change. You can worry about whether you will be able to maintain your newfound truth. You anticipate future events and worry about how you will navigate your authenticity when the time comes. But being your authentic self is a moment-by-moment existence. It's about who you are right now and what you are doing and feeling now. Not later, not before. Now is who you are. It's all you are. It's all you can be. Later you'll be someone else, and you'll have to wait until then to see who it is because that future moment is different to now, and you have no idea what it will contain and what you will be up against. So don't bother trying to prepare yourself for it, to predict it, or make promises for it.

Because, right now, I know that what I'm doing is aligned with the highest version of myself. That's the best I can do. I'm not worried about the next moment and whether I'll still be as authentic then. I'm not worried about the last moment when I had an inauthentic moment. Worrying about those things isn't in my preapproved list of higher order behaviours that will align me with my highest self, so worrying about the past or the future in that way will only serve to diminish my authenticity in the now.

At this moment in time, I'm a calm, placid person drinking green tea. Tomorrow, you could bring me a green tea and I might say, "What's with the green tea? I'm going out. Give me a Red Bull and call me an Uber." That's living in the moment. And that's totally cool.

So, given the now is all you've got any control over, be yourself now and fuck the rest.

A NOTE FROM ME TO YOU

You have started this awakening, and I would love to connect with you, to get to know you and walk alongside you as you explore this new path. Come join me on Instagram or visit my website, and we can celebrate your wins, your epiphanies, and your discoveries together. Reach out if there's anything more you need. There's so much more where this came from, I could bask in it all day long.

Cartoon by Michael Leunig, 1988

Keep farting.

ABOUT THE AUTHOR

Kate lives on Ngunnawal land in the Australian Capital Territory. She is the founder of Your Light Side initiative and is a business architect with the Australian government, where she turns up on time, wears high heels, and asks a lot of questions. She has a postgraduate degree in psychology—which has recently really come in handy—and has started to dabble in energetics and Human Design. She likes talking to people about what they would rather be doing, hanging out in the bush, and never passes up an opportunity for a swim. When she is not exploring the countryside barefoot, she is at home with her husband, her two teenage sons, and the Manchurian pear tree that lives out the back.

For more information about Kate and her current antics, visit:

Instagram: kateangel.yourlightside
Youtube.com/@yourlightside
kateangel.com

www.ingramcontent.com/pod-product-compliance
Lightning Source LLC
Chambersburg PA
CBHW020352130626
46549CB00006B/2274